Frogs

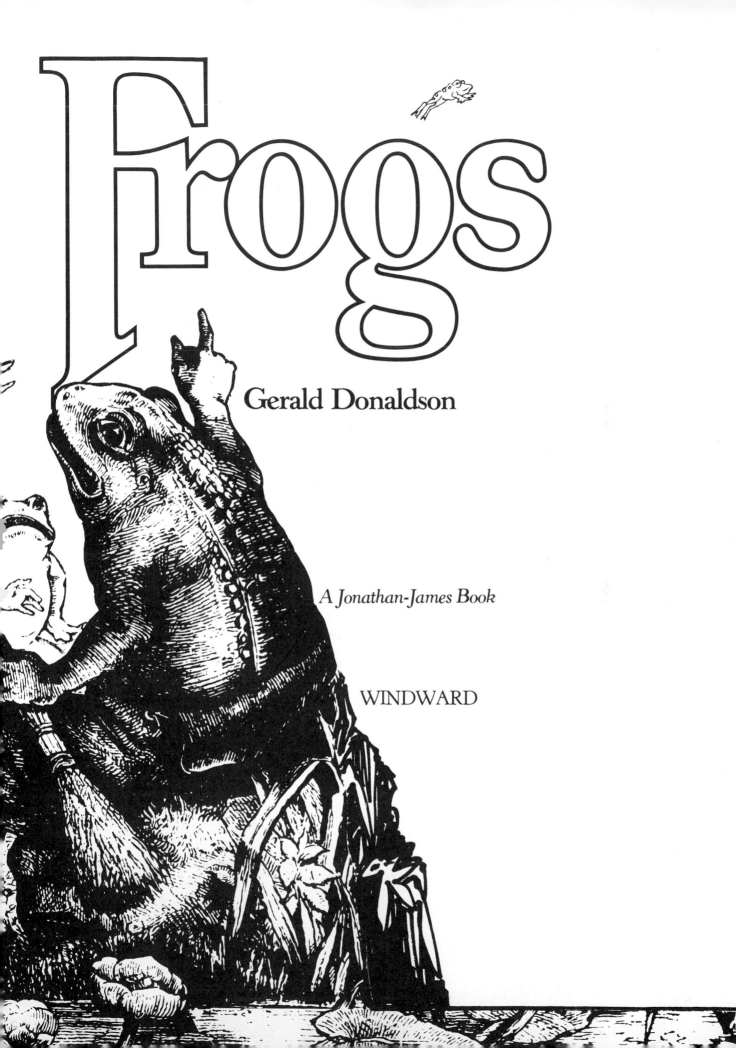

Frogs

Gerald Donaldson

A Jonathan-James Book

WINDWARD

ISBN 0 7112 0037 8

Windward
An imprint owned by:
W.H. Smith and Son Ltd.
Registered No. 237811 England
Trading as:
W.H.S. Distributors
Euston Street
Freeman's Common
Aylestone Road
Leicester LE2 7SS

Created and produced by:
Jonathan-James Books
5 Sultan Street
Toronto, Ontario
Canada M5S 1L6

Edited by Katherine Koller
Designed by Maher & Murtagh

Printed in the United States of America

Acknowledgements

The author would like to thank the following sources for kind permission to include textual excerpts in this book: Blackie & Sons Ltd. for "The Frog and the Bird" by Vera Hessey from *In Poem Town III*; George Braziller, Inc. for "The Frogs" by Jules Renard from *Natural Histories*; Cambridge University Press for "Dialogue" from *Moorish Poetry* translated by Arberry; Constable Publishers and Desmond Elliott for "The Frog Race" by Leslie Thomas from *The Virgin Soldiers*; Doubleday & Company Inc. for poems from *An Introduction to Haiku* by Harold G. Henderson, Copyright© 1958 by Harold G. Henderson; Dover Publications, Inc. for "Mutual Respect" by Christina Rossetti from *Sing Song*; Evans Brothers Ltd. for "The Brown Frog" by Mary K. Robinson from *Book of a Thousand Poems*; Eyre Methuen Ltd. for "St. Benno and the Frog" by Fougasse from *An Animal Anthology* and for "Across the Andes by Frog" from *Bert Fegg's Nasty Book for Boys and Girls* by Terry Jones and Michael Palin; Harvard University Press and the Trustees of Amherst College for poems by Emily Dickinson, reprinted by permission from *The Poems of Emily Dickinson,* edited by Thomas H. Johnson, Cambridge, Mass.: The Belknap Press of Harvard University Press, Copyright© 1951, 1955 by the President and Fellows of Harvard College; David Higham Associates Ltd. for "The Evolution of Frog Knowledge"ifrom *The Book of Beasts* by T. H. White; The Hogarth Press Ltd. for an excerpt from "Surroundings" by Norman MacCaig from *A Book of Animal Poems*; Little, Brown and Company for an excerpt from "The Long Sigh of the Frog" from *The Complete Poems of Emily*

Dickinson edited by Thomas H. Johnson, Copyright© 1914, 1942 by Martha Dickinson Bianchi; Longman Cheshire Pty. Ltd. for "The Frog Plague" from *Condolences of the Season* by Bruce Dawe; James MacGibbon and Oxford University Press, New York for "The Frog Prince" from *The Collected Poems of Stevie Smith* by Stevie Smith; Macmillan London Ltd. for "A Strange Ceremony" from *The Golden Bough* by James Frazer; McClelland and Stewart Ltd., Toronto, for "Frog Cantatas" by Joe Rosenblatt from *Virgins and Vampires*; Norma Millay for "Assault" from *Collected Poems,* Harper & Row, Publishers, Copyright© 1921, 1948 by Edna St. Vincent Millay; Iona and Peter Opie for "The Frog and the Crow" from *A Family Book of Nursery Rhymes,* Oxford University Press, Copyright© 1964 by Iona and Peter Opie; Oxford University Press for "The Lovesick Frog" from *The Oxford Nursery Rhyme Book* compiled by Iona and Peter Opie; Random House, Inc. and Gerald Duckworth & Company Ltd. for "The Frog" by Hilaire Belloc from *Cautionary Verses*; University of California Press for six haiku from *The Year of My Life: A Translation of Issa's Oraga Haru* by Nobuyuki Yuasa, Copyright© 1960, 1972 by The Regents of the University of California, reprinted by permission of the University of California Press; The University of Chicago Press for "The Frog that Rode Snakeback" from *The Panchantantra* translated by Arthur Ryder, Copyright© 1925 by The University of Chicago Press; Viking Penguin Inc. for poems from *Frogs and Others* by Kusan Shimpei, reprinted by permission, all rights reserved; Wesleyan University Press for "Frogs" from *At the End of the*

Open Road by Louis Simpson, Copyright© 1963 by Louis Simpson.

The author would also like to thank the following for permission to include illustrations in this book: Ron Berg; Dover Publications, Inc.; The Hamlyn Group; Eleanor Kanasawe, by permission of Frank Meawasige, Woodland Studios; Kim La Fave; The Mansell Collection; Mary Evans Picture Library; Metropolitan Toronto Library Board; Osborne Collection of Early Children's Books; Anna Pugh; Royal Ontario Museum; Anton Seder; Smithsonian Institution, Freer Gallery of Art, Washington, D.C.; Victoria and Albert Museum, Crown Copyright; Yale University Library, New Haven, Connecticut.

The author would also like to thank the following frogophiles for their help in preparing this book: David Allen and Joseph Duff in Toronto and Jessica Strang in London for original photography; Elizabeth James and Timothy O'Grady for research in London; Howard Kaplan of The International Thrinberry Corp. and Frog Sanctuary, Toronto; Pat Rogal of The Metropolitan Toronto Library; Margaret Maloney of The Osborne Collection of Early Children's Books, Toronto Public Library; and Elizabeth Donaldson.

Contents

1
Wonderful Wisdom of Frogs

Fables, fairy tales, poems and pictures showing their inherent intelligence, how they can hold their own with any other creatures, including men, and their influence over the powers-that-be on earth and elsewhere.

2
Follies and Foibles of Frogs

Art, legends and songs that expose their woeful weaknesses, complicated love-lives and blind ambitions in their natural environment and in some of the most unusual places, including the moon.

3
Mysterious Power of Frogs

Fact and fiction selected from the f corners of the world to reveal secre of their strange inner strengths together with several examples of certain miraculous capabilities that defy explanation.

4
Trials and Tribulations of Frogs

Chronicles of their terrible sufferin at the hands of men and others who would use them for personal gain and some of the dastardly crimes committed against them in the nam of science, advertising and literatur

5
Strange Encounters with Frogs

Historical accounts of astonishing confrontations that show the awesome toll of revenge exacted against their enemies and some terrifying reports of the ways in which they can strike fear into the soul.

6
Private Lives of Frogs

Revelations of natural and unnatural occurrences as found in diaries, theses and poems that afford intimate glimpses into their often curious behavior as well as insights into their everyday personalities.

7
Symbolism and Meaning of Frogs

Attempts to explain and analyze thousands of years of preoccupation with frogs and their very special place in religion, mythology, the natural order of things and in the hearts and minds of men.

1 Wonderful Wisdom of Frogs

My hermitage:
The frogs here, from the very start
have chanted of old age.

– Issa

The Frog

Once upon a time there was a woman who had three sons. Though they were peasants they were well off, for the soil on which they lived was fruitful, and yielded rich crops. One day they all three told their mother they meant to get married. To which their mother replied: "Do as you like, but see that you choose good housewives, who will look carefully after your affairs; and, to make certain of this, take with you these three skeins of flax, and give it to them to spin. Whoever spins the best will be my favourite daughter-in-law."

Now the two eldest sons had already chosen their wives; so they took the flax from their mother, and carried it off with them, to have it spun as she had said. But the youngest son was puzzled what to do with his skein, as he knew no girl (never having spoken to any) to whom he could give it to be spun. He wandered hither and thither, asking the girls that he met if they would undertake the task for him, but at the sight of the flax they laughed in his face and mocked at him. Then in despair he left their villages, and went out into the country, and seating himself on the bank of a pond began to cry bitterly.

Suddenly there was a noise close beside him, and a frog jumped out of the water on to the bank and asked him why he was crying. The youth told her of his trouble, and how his brothers would bring home linen spun for them by their promised wives, but that no one would spin his thread.

Then the frog answered: "Do not weep on that account; give me the thread, and I will spin it for you." And, having said this, she took it out of his hand, and flopped back into the water, and the youth went back, not knowing what would happen next.

In a short time the two elder brothers came home, and their mother asked to see the linen which had been woven out of the skeins of flax she had given them. They all three left the room; and in a few minutes the two eldest returned, bringing with them the linen that had been spun by their chosen wives. But the youngest brother was greatly troubled, for he had nothing to show for the skein of flax that had been given to him. Sadly he betook himself to the pond, and sitting down on the bank, began to weep.

Flop! and the frog appeared out of the water close beside him.

"Take this," she said; "here is the linen that I have spun for you."

You may imagine how delighted the youth was. She put the linen into his hands, and he took it straight back to his mother, who was so pleased with it that she declared she had never seen linen so beautifully spun, and that it was far finer and whiter than the webs that the two elder brothers had brought home.

Then she returned to her sons and said: "But this is not enough, my sons, I must have another proof as to what sort of wives you have chosen. In the house there

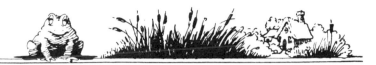

are three puppies. Each of you take one, and give it to the woman whom you mean to bring home as your wife. She must train it and bring it up. Whichever dog turns out the best, its mistress will be my favourite daughter-in-law."

So the young men set out on their different ways, each taking a puppy with him. The youngest, not knowing where to go, returned to the pond, sat down once more on the bank, and began to weep.

Flop! and close beside him, he saw the frog. "Why are you weeping?" she said. Then he told her his difficulty, and that he did not know to whom he should take the puppy.

"Give it to me," she said, "and I will bring it up for you." And, seeing that the youth hesitated, she took the little creature out of his arms, and disappeared with it into the pond.

The weeks and months passed, till one day the mother said she would like to see how the dogs had been trained by her future daughters-in-law. The two eldest sons departed, and returned shortly, leading with them two great mastiffs, who growled so fiercely, and looked so savage, that the mere sight of them made the mother tremble with fear.

The youngest son, as was his custom, went to the pond, and called on the frog to come to his rescue.

In a minute she was at his side, bringing with her the most lovely little dog, which she put into his arms. It sat up and begged with its paws, and went through the prettiest tricks, and was almost human in the way it understood and did what it was told.

In high spirits the youth carried it off to his mother. As soon as she saw it, she exclaimed: "This is the most beautiful little dog I have ever seen. You are indeed fortunate, my son; you have won a pearl of a wife."

Then, turning to the others, she said: "Here are three shirts; take them to your chosen wives. Whoever sews the best will be my favourite daughter-in-law."

So the young men set out once more; and again, this time, the work of the frog was much the best and the neatest.

This time the mother said: "Now that I am content with the tests I gave, I want you to go and fetch home your brides, and I will prepare the wedding-feast."

You may imagine what the youngest brother felt on hearing these words. Whence was he to fetch a bride? Would the frog be able to help him in this new difficulty? With bowed head, and feeling very sad, he sat down on the edge of the pond.

Flop! and once more the faithful frog was beside him.

"What is troubling you so much?" she asked him, and then the youth told her everything.

"Will you take me for a wife?" she asked.

"What should I do with you as a wife?" he replied, wondering at her strange proposal.

"Once more, will you have me or will you not?" she said.

"I will neither have you, nor will I refuse you," said he.

At this the frog disappeared; and the next minute the youth beheld a lovely little chariot, drawn by two tiny ponies, standing on the road. The frog was holding the carriage door open for him to step in.

"Come with me," she said. And he got up and followed her into the chariot. As they drove along the road they met three witches; the first of them was blind, the second was hunchbacked, and the third had a large thorn in her throat. When the three witches beheld the chariot, the frog seated pompously among the cushions, they broke into such fits of laughter that the eyelids of the blind one burst open, and she recovered her sight; the hunchback rolled about on the ground in merriment till her back became straight, and in a roar of laughter the thorn fell out of the throat of the third witch. Their first thought was to reward the frog, who had unconsciously been the means of curing them of their misfortunes. The first witch waved her magic wand over the frog, and changed her into the loveliest girl that had ever been seen. The second witch waved the wand over the tiny chariot and ponies, and they were turned into a beautiful carriage with prancing horses, and a coachman on the seat. The third witch gave the girl a magic purse, filled with money.

Having done this, the witches disappeared, and the youth with his lovely bride drove to his mother's home. Great was the delight of the mother at her youngest son's good fortune. A beautiful house was built for them; she was the favourite daughter-in-law; and everything went well with them, and they lived happily ever after.

– An Italian Fairy Tale

The Merry Frogs

This is a story told by the Coras, those strange Indians who live in the mountains of Nayarit and Jalisco in Mexico. On their tiny guitars and violins that are like toys, they play wild music that sounds like that of the Chinese. They wear long hair, bound back from their eyes with home-woven fillets of beautiful design. From a great distance they can shoot a rabbit or deer with their fleet-winged arrows.

These Coras worship the fire and the sun, and work hard, fasting, praying, and "making *mitote,*" dances to call the rain from the clouds to bless their country and make it green with corn.

In the times of the ancients there came a season when for many days no rain fell. Everything grew dry and dusty. The ground became hard and cracked open. Nothing would grow. The people knew that unless the corn could grow, they would have no food and would starve.

The five principal men called the humming birds to them.

"Go," they commanded them, "to the place in the east where the rain-clouds live. Ask them to come over here."

The humming birds darted out, flying very swiftly across the sky, as swiftly as lightning, with their whirring wings humming around them in flashes of brilliant color. When the clouds saw the humming birds, they came out of their homes in the east, and they killed the messengers that had come to them from the ancients.

They killed them and stole their beautiful robes of bright-colored feathers. To this day, when it rains, you can sometimes see a procession across the sky, a procession of the thieves dressed in the humming birds' robes. We call the parade a rainbow.

When the clouds had stolen the humming birds' robes, they ran back to their caves in the east.

After a while the humming birds came to life again. They had to go to all of the flowers, their friends, and borrow colors to make new robes.

When they were dressed again, they returned to the ancients and told them that they had called the clouds, but the clouds, after treating them very badly, had returned to their caves.

The people asked who would go now as messengers. No one wanted to volunteer. They were all afraid.

The Frog came late to the meeting. When it was explained to him what had happened, he croaked quickly, "I will go. My five sons and I will go, for there is nothing we fear!"

The ancients then sent out the Frog with his five sons.

As the Frog went toward the east, on each mountain he left one of his sons. When he came to the last mountain, he hallowed loudly, calling the clouds, and then he began to run back.

The clouds chased him quickly across the mountain, but as they were about to catch him he hid himself under a stone. The clouds not seeing him hurried on.

Then the fifth son called them, as he began to run back across his mountain top. Seeing him they thought he was his father and began to chase him. When they were about to overtake him, he too quickly hid himself under a stone, and the clouds rolled on.

The fourth son on his mountain began to call them, then ran and hid; the third son did the same, and so did the second and first.

In that way the clouds came at last to a mountain so far on the west of the sierra that the sea may be seen from it.

That is how the rain came to the land of the ancients.

When the rain was over and the storm-clouds went away again, back to their caves in the east of the sky (not, however, without a great deal of grumbling and thundering) the frogs began to sing merrily.

And to this very day, when rain is coming to the Cora country the frogs hide under stones, for they know the clouds cannot forgive them that old trick. And when the clouds leave again, to this very time the frogs sing merrily the day after the rain.

– A Legend of the Cora Indians (as told by Idella Purnell)

O to be a frog, my lads, and live aloof from care.

– Theocritus, 3rd Century B.C.

The Gnome and the Frog

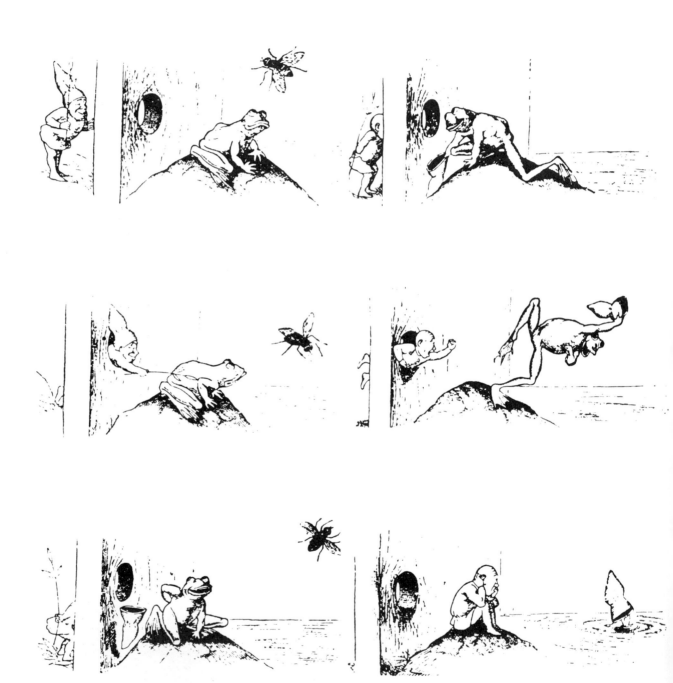

The Frogs Praise God

After the maggid's death, his disciples came together and talked about the things he had done. When it was Rabbi Schneur Zalman's turn, he asked them: "Do you know why our master went to the pond every day at dawn and stayed there for a little while before coming home again?" They did not know why. Rabbi Zalman continued: "He was learning the song with which the frogs praise God. It takes a very long time to learn that song."

– Martin Buber, *Tales of the Hasidim, Early Masters*

There are not frogs wherever
    there is water; but
Wherever there are frogs, water
    will be found.

– Goethe, *Sprüche in Prosa*

A frog would leap from a throne of gold into a puddle.

– Publius Syrus, *Moral Sayings*

The Two Frogs

Two frogs dwelt in the same pool. The pool being dried up under the summer's heat, they left it, and set out together to seek another home. As they went along they chanced to pass a deep well, amply supplied with water, on seeing which one of the Frogs said to the other; "Let us descend and make our abode in this well, it will furnish us with shelter and food." The other replied with greater caution; "But suppose the water should fail us, how can we get out again from so great a depth?" (Do nothing without a regard to the consequences.)

– Aesop

The Frog's Saddle Horse

Once upon a time the Elephant and the Frog went courting the same girl, and at last she promised to marry the Elephant. One day the Frog said to her: "That Elephant is nothing but my saddle horse."

When the Elephant came to call that night the girl said to him: "You are nothing but the Frog's saddle horse!"

When he heard this the Elephant went off at once and found the Frog, and asked him: "Did you tell the girl that I am nothing but your saddle horse?"

"Oh, no, indeed," said the Frog. "I never told her that!"

Thereupon they both started back together to see the girl. On the way the Frog said: "Grandpa Elephant, I am too tired to walk any further. Let me climb up on your back."

"Certainly," said the Elephant. "Climb up, my grandson." So the Frog climbed up on the Elephant's back. Presently he said: "Grandpa Elephant, I am afraid that I am going to fall off. Let me take some little chords and fasten them to your tusks, to hold on by."

"Certainly, my grandson," said the Elephant; and he stood still while the Frog did as he had asked. Presently the Frog spoke again: "Grandpa Elephant, please stop and let me pick a green branch so that I can keep the flies off of you."

"Certainly, my grandson," said the Elephant, and he stood quite still while the Frog broke off the branch. Pretty soon they drew near to the house where the girl lived. And when she saw them coming, the Elephant plodding patiently along with the little Frog perched on his broad back, holding the cords in one hand and waving the green branch, she came to meet them, calling: "Mr. Elephant, you certainly are nothing but the Frog's saddle horse!"

– An Asian Fable

The Frogs Frightened at the Battle of the Bulls

A Frog, viewing from a marsh a combat of some Bulls, "Alas!" said she, "what terrible destruction is threatening us!" Being asked by another why she said so, as the Bulls were contending for the sovereignty of the herd, and passed their lives far from them, "Their habitation is at a distance," said she, "and they are of a different kind; still, he who is expelled from the sovereignty of the meadow will take to flight, and come to the secret hiding-places in the fens, and trample and crush us with his hard hoofs. Thus does their fury concern our safety."

– Phaedrus

The Frog Prince

I am a frog
I live under a spell
I live at the bottom
Of a green well

And here I must wait
Until a maiden places me
On her royal pillow
And kisses me
In her father's palace.

The story is familiar
Everybody knows it well
But do other enchanted people feel as nervous
As I do? The stories do not tell,

Ask if they will be happier
When the changes come
As already they are fairly happy
In a frog's doom?

I have been a frog now
For a hundred years
And in all this time
I have not shed many tears,

I am happy, I like the life,
Can swim for many a mile
(When I have hopped to the river)
And am for ever agile.

And the quietness,
Yes, I like to be quiet
I am habituated
To a quiet life,

But always when I think these thoughts
As I sit in my well
Another thought comes to me and says:
It is part of the spell

To be happy
To work up contentment
To make much of being a frog
To fear disenchantment

Says, It will be *heavenly*
To be set free,
Cries, *Heavenly* the girl who disenchants
And the royal times, *heavenly*,
And I think it will be.

Come, then, royal girl and royal times,
Come quickly,
I can be happy until you come
But I cannot be heavenly,
Only disenchanted people
Can be heavenly.

– Stevie Smith

Frogs at School

The sun was shining softly,
The day was calm and cool,
When forty-five frog scholars met
Down by the shady pool.
Poor little frogs, like little folk,
Are always sent to school.

Their lessons seemed the strangest things:
They learned that grapes were sour;
They learned that four-and-twenty days
Exactly made an hour;
That bricks were made of houses,
And corn was made of flour;

That six times one was ninety-five,
And "yes" meant "no" or "nay";
They always spent to-morrow
Before they spent to-day;
While each commenced the alphabet
With Z instead of A.

As soon as school was over,
The master said: "No noise!
Now go and play at leap-frog"
(The game a frog enjoys),
"And mind that you behave yourselves,
And don't throw stones at boys."

– Anonymous

The Frog and the Two Fish

In a certain reservoir were two fishes, one named Satabuddhi, or the hundred-witted, the other Sahasrabuddhi or the thousand-witted. They had a friend, a frog, named Ekabuddhi or the single-wit, with whom they were in the habit of meeting and conversing at the edge of the water. When the usual party assembled, they saw several fishermen approach with their nets, and heard them say to one another, "This pool is full of fish, the water is but shallow; we will come to-morrow morning and drag it." They then went away. When they had departed, the frog said to his friends, "What is to be done, had we not better make our escape?" at which the thousand-witted laughed and said, "Never fear, they have only talked of coming. Yet if they should come I will be answerable for your safety as well as my own. I shall be a match for them as I know all the courses of the water." The hundred-witted one said, "My friend here is very right; wherever there is a way for the breeze, for water or its tenants, or for the rays of the sun, the intellect of a sagacious person will penetrate. By following his counsel your life would be in no peril, even had you approached the abodes of the manes. Stay where you are, even I will undertake your safety." The frog said, "I have perhaps but limited talent, a mere singleness of sense, but that tells me to flee, and therefore whilst I can I shall withdraw with my mate to another piece of water." The frog left the pool that night. In the morning the fishermen arrived, and the lake was so beset with nets that all the fish, turtles, crabs, and other tenants of the water, were made prisoners, and amongst them Satabuddhi and Sahasrabuddhi, in spite of their boasted cunning, were caught and killed. The frog saw the fishermen on their return, and recognising Satabuddhi on the head of one man, and Sahasrabuddhi dragged along with cords by another, he pointed them out to his mate, saying, "See where Satabuddhi or the hundred-witted one is carried on the head, and there also is Sahasrabuddhi or the thousand-witted one, whilst I, who am Ekabuddhi or the single-wit, still can gambol in the crystal stream."

– The Panchatantra, circa 200 B.C.

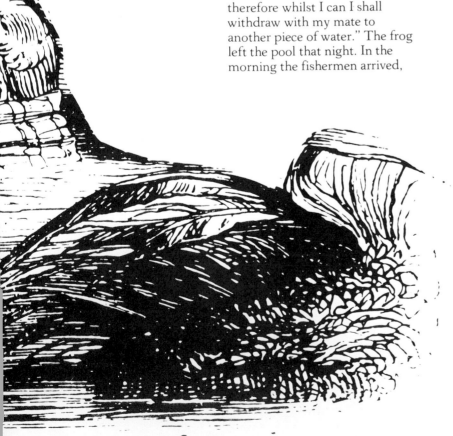

2 Follies and Foibles of Frogs

*The frog looks as if
He had just belched
A misty cloud
Into the sky.*

– Issa

The Frogs that Rode Snakeback

Bear even foes upon your back;
When fortune clogs
Your path, endure. The great black snake
Slew many frogs.

There was once an elderly black snake in a certain spot, and his name was Slow-Poison. He considered the situation from this point of view: "How in the world can I get along without overtaxing my energies?" Then he went to a pond containing many frogs, and behaved as if very dejected.

As he waited thus, a frog came to the edge of the water and asked: "Uncle, why don't you bustle about today for food as usual?"

"My dear friend," said Slow-Poison, "I am afflicted. Why should I wish for food? For this evening, as I was bustling about for food, I saw a frog and made ready to catch him. But he saw me

and, fearing death, he escaped among some Brahmans intent upon holy recitation, nor did I perceive which way he went. But in the water at the edge of the pond was the great toe of a Brahman boy, and stupidly deceived by its resemblance to a frog, I bit it, and the boy died immediately. Then the sorrowing father cursed me in these terms: 'Monster! Since you bit my harmless son, you shall for this sin become a vehicle for frogs, and shall subsist on whatever they choose to allow you.' Consequently, I have come here to serve as your vehicle."

Now the frog reported this to all the others. And every last one of them, in extreme delight, went and reported to the frog-king, whose name was Water-Foot. He in turn, accompanied by his counselors, rose hurriedly from the pond — for he thought it an extraordinary occurrence — and climbed upon Slow-Poison's hood. The others also, in order of age, climbed on his back. Yet others, finding no vacant spot, hopped along behind the snake. Now Slow-Poison, with an eye to making his living, showed them fancy turns in great variety. And Water-Foot, enjoying contact with his body, said to him:

> I'd rather ride Slow-Poison than
> The finest horse I've seen,
> Or elephant, or chariot
> Or man-borne palanquin.

The next day, Slow-Poison was wily enough to move very slowly. So Water-Foot said: "My dear Slow-Poison, why don't you carry us nicely, as you did before?"

And Slow-Poison said: "O King, I have no carrying power today because of lack of food." "My dear fellow," said the king, "eat the plebeian frogs."

When Slow-Poison heard this, he quivered with joy in every member and made haste to say: "Why, that is a part of the curse laid on me by the Brahman. For that reason I am greatly pleased at your command." So he ate frogs uninterruptedly, and in a very few days he grew strong. And with delight and inner laughter, he said:

> The trick was good. All sorts of frogs
> Within my power have passed.
> The only question that remains,
> Is: How long will they last?

Water-Foot, for his part, was befooled by Slow-Poison's plausibilities, and did not notice a thing.

– *The Panchatantra*

The Funny Frog

Of all the funny things that live
In woodland, marsh or bog.
That creep the ground or fly the air,
The funniest thing's the frog.

– Anonymous, *The Scientific Frog,* circa 1812

The Frog Bird

What a wonderful bird the frog are.
When he sit, he stand almost;
When he flop, he fly almost.
He ain't got no sense hardly.
He ain't got no tail hardly either.
When he sit, he sit on what he ain't got almost.

– Anonymous

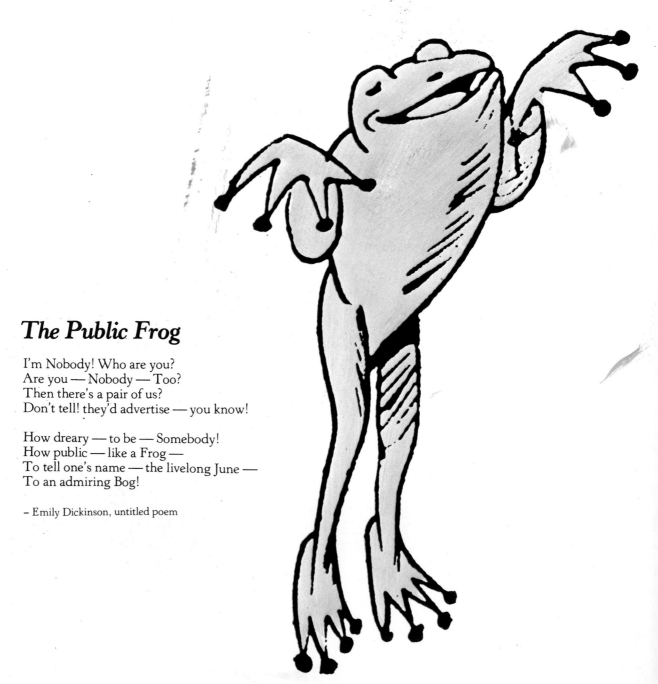

The Public Frog

I'm Nobody! Who are you?
Are you — Nobody — Too?
Then there's a pair of us?
Don't tell! they'd advertise — you know!

How dreary — to be — Somebody!
How public — like a Frog —
To tell one's name — the livelong June —
To an admiring Bog!

– Emily Dickinson, untitled poem

The Frog and the Ox

As a splendid Ox — who, by right of the great family he belonged to, was permitted to disport himself as he pleased in the fashionable parks of London — was taking his afternoon stroll, an envious, tawdry-coated little Frog, that stood gaping at him hardby, called out to certain of his fellows (who had hopped thither in his company all the way from the Fleet Ditch in the City), to take particular notice of the enormous size of the first-mentioned animal.

"And see," he said, "if I don't make the biggest swell of the two." So he puffed himself up, once, twice, and again, and went still swelling on in impotent emulation, till in the end, — in spite of the cautions of his brother frogs — he burst himself.

MORAL
The humble citizen who strives, by mere inflation, to make as great an outward appearance as his substantial neighbour, must inevitably go to pieces.

– Aesop

A Frog Love Triangle

– Heinrich Kley

The Two Frogs

Once upon a time in the country of Japan there lived two frogs, one of whom made his home in a ditch near the town of Osaka, on the sea coast, while the other dwelt in a clear little stream which ran through the city of Kioto. At such a great distance apart, they had never even heard of each other; but, funnily enough, the idea came into both their heads at once that they should like to see a little of the world, and the frog who lived at Kioto wanted to visit Osaka, and the frog who lived at Osaka wished to go to Kioto, where the great Mikado had his palace.

So one fine morning in the spring they both set out along the road that led from Kioto to Osaka, one from one end and the other from the other. The journey was more tiring than they expected, for they did not know much about travelling, and half way between the two towns there arose a mountain which had to be climbed. It took them a long time and a great many hops to reach the top, but there they were at last, and what was the surprise of each to see another frog before him! They looked at each other for a moment without speaking, and then fell into conversation, explaining the cause of their meeting so far from their homes. It was delightful to find that they both felt the same wish — to learn a little more of their native country — and as there was no sort of hurry they stretched themselves out in a cool, damp place, and agreed that they would have a good rest before they parted to go their ways.

"What a pity we are not bigger," said the Osaka frog; "for then we could see both towns from here, and tell if it is worth our while going on."

"Oh, that is easily managed," returned the Kioto frog. "We have only got to stand up on our hind legs, and hold on to each other, and then we can each look at the town he is travelling to."

This idea pleased the Osaka frog so much that he at once jumped up and put his front paws on the shoulders of his friend, who had risen also. There they both stood, stretching themselves as high as they could, and holding each other tightly, so that they might not fall down. The Kioto frog turned his nose towards Osaka, and the Osaka frog turned his nose towards Kioto; but the foolish things forgot that when they stood up their great eyes lay in the backs of their heads, and that though their noses might point to the places to which they wanted to go their eyes beheld the places from which they had come.

"Dear me!" cried the Osaka frog, "Kioto is exactly like Osaka. It is certainly not worth such a long journey. I shall go home!"

"If I had had any idea that Osaka was only a copy of Kioto I should never have travelled all this way," exclaimed the frog from Kioto, and as he spoke he took his hands from his friend's shoulders, and they both fell down on the grass. Then they took a polite farewell of each other, and set off for home again, and to the end of their lives they believed that Osaka and Kioto, which are as different to look at as two towns can be, were as like as two peas.

– A Japanese Fable

A Frog in a String Quartet

Joseph Haydn composed his Quartet Number 49 in D Major for two violins, viola and violoncello in 1785. For the most part it is a thoughtful and serious work but in Opus 50, Number 6, a frog can be heard croaking loudly, even stridently, in sounds produced by playing the same notes alternately on two neighbouring strings. This part of the set is popularly known as The Frog.

The Hare and the Frogs

A hare one day sat meditating on his own excessive timidity. It was a sad thing, he reflected, to have such weak nerves. He was always in alarm about something; a breath of wind or a passing shadow would throw him into a fever. It happened, however, shortly afterwards, that, as he was passing a pond, the frogs leapt in, greatly alarmed at his appearance, and hid themselves in the mud at the bottom. "Oh, oh!" cried he, "then there are creatures as much afraid of me as I am afraid of men! These animals tremble at my approach. I am to them a thunderbolt of war."

– La Fontaine

The Lovesick Frog

A frog he would a-wooing go,
Heigh ho! says Rowley,
Whether his mother would let him or no.
With a rowley, powley, gammon and spinach,
Heigh ho! says Anthony Rowley.

So off he set with his opera hat,
Heigh ho! says Rowley,
And on the road he met with a rat.
With a rowley, powley, gammon and spinach,
Heigh ho! says Anthony Rowley.

Pray, Mister Rat, will you go with me?
Heigh ho! says Rowley.
Kind Mistress Mousey for to see?
With a rowley, powley, gammon and spinach,
Heigh ho! says Anthony Rowley.

They came to the door of Mousey's hall
Heigh ho! says Rowley,
They gave a loud knock, and they gave a loud call.
With a rowley, powley, gammon and spinach,
Heigh ho! says Anthony Rowley.

Pray, Mistress Mouse, are you within?
Heigh ho! says Rowley,
Oh yes, kind sirs, I'm sitting to spin.
With a rowley, powley, gammon and spinach,
Heigh ho! says Anthony Rowley.

Pray, Mistress Mouse, will you give us some beer?
Heigh ho! says Rowley,
For Froggy and I are fond of good cheer.
With a rowley, powley, gammon and spinach,
Heigh ho! says Anthony Rowley.

Pray, Mister Frog, will you give us a song?
Heigh ho! says Rowley,
Let it be something that's not very long.
With a rowley, powley, gammon and spinach,
Heigh ho! says Anthony Rowley.

Indeed, Mistress House, replied Mister Frog,
Heigh ho! says Rowley,
A cold has made me as hoarse as a dog.
With a rowley, powley, gammon and spinach,
Heigh ho! says Anthony Rowley.

Since you have a cold, Mister Frog, Mousey said,
Heigh ho! says Rowley,
I'll sing you a song that I have just made.
With a rowley, powley, gammon and spinach,
Heigh ho! says Anthony Rowley.

But while they were all a-merring-making,
Heigh ho! says Rowley,
A cat and her kittens came tumbling in.
With a rowley, powley, gammon and spinach,
Heigh ho! says Anthony Rowley.

The cat she seized the rat by the crown,
Heigh ho! says Rowley,
The kittens they pulled the little mouse down.
With a rowley, powley, gammon and spinach,
Heigh ho! says Anthony Rowley.

This put Mister Frog in a terrible fright,
Heigh ho! says Rowley,
He took up his hat and he wished them good-night.
With a rowley, powley, gammon and spinach,
Heigh ho! says Anthony Rowley.

But as Froggy was crossing over a brook,
Heigh ho! says Rowley,
A lily-white duck came and gobbled him up.
With a rowley, powley, gammon and spinach,
Heigh ho! says Anthony Rowley.

So there was an end of one, two, three
Heigh ho! says Rowley,
The rat, the mouse, and the little frog-ee.
With a rowley, powley, gammon and spinach,
Heigh ho! says Anthony Rowley.

The Frogs Asking for a King

In the days of old, when the frogs were all at liberty in the lakes, and had grown quite weary of following every one his own devices, they assembled one day together, and with no little clamour petitioned Jupiter to let them have a King to keep them in better order, and make them lead more honest lives. Jupiter, knowing the vanity of their hearts, smiled at their request, and threw down a Log into the lake, which by the splash and commotion it made, sent the whole commonwealth into the greatest terror and amazement. They rushed under the water and into the mud, and dared not come within ten leaps' length of the spot where it lay.

At length one Frog bolder than the rest ventured to pop his head above the water, and take a survey of their new King at a respectful distance. Presently, when they perceived the Log lie stock-still, others began to swim up to it and around it; till by degrees, growing bolder and bolder, they at last leaped upon it, and treated it with the greatest contempt.

Dissatisfied with so tame a ruler, they forthwith petitioned Jupiter a second time for another and more active King. Upon which he sent them a Stork, who no sooner arrived among them than he began laying hold of them and devouring them one by one as fast as he could, and it was in vain that they endeavoured to escape him.

Then they sent Mercury with a private message to Jupiter, beseeching him that he would take pity on them once more; but Jupiter replied, that they were only suffering the punishment due to their folly, and that another time they would learn to let well alone, and not be dissatisfied with their natural condition.

– Aesop

The frog's own croak betrays him.

– Old Proverb

Ido no Kawazu taikai wo shirazu: A frog in the well knows not of the ocean.

– Japanese Proverb

Gomame no hagishiri: The frog flew into a passion and the pond knew nothing about it.

– Japanese Proverb

The Man in the Moon

The three Frog sisters had a house in a swamp, where they lived together. Not very far away lived a number of people in another house. Among them were Snake and Beaver, who were friends. They were well-grown lads, and wished to marry the Frog girls.

One night Snake went to Frog's house, and, crawling up to one of the sisters, put his hand on her face. She awoke, and asked him who he was. Learning that he was Snake, she said she would not marry him, and told him to leave at once. She called him hard names, such as, "slimy-fellow,"

"small-eyes," etc. Snake returned, and told his friend of his failure.

Next night Beaver went to try, and, crawling up to one of the sisters, he put his hand on her face. She awoke, and, finding out who he was, she told him to be gone. She called him names, such as, "short-legs," "big-belly," "big-buttocks." Beaver felt hurt, and, going home, began to cry. His father asked him what the matter was, and the boy told him. He said, "That is nothing. Don't cry! It will rain too much." But young Beaver said, "I *will* cry."

As he continued to cry, much rain fell, and soon the swamp where the Frogs lived was flooded. Their house was under the water, which covered the tops of the tall swamp grass. The Frogs got cold, and went to Beaver's house, and said to him, "We wish to marry your sons." But old Beaver said, "No! You called us hard names."

The water was now running in a regular stream. So the Frogs swam away downstream until they reached a whirlpool, which sucked them in, and they descended to the house of the Moon. The latter invited them to warm themselves at the fire; but they said, "No. We do not wish to sit by the fire. We wish to sit there," pointing at him. He said, "Here?" at the same time pointing to his feet. They said, "No, not there." Then he pointed to one part of his body after another, until he reached his brow. When he said, "Will you sit here?" they all cried out, "Yes," and jumped on his face, thus spoiling his beauty. The Frog sisters may be seen on the moon's face at the present day.

– A Legend of the Lillooet Tribe of North America

The Frog and the Bird

By a quiet little stream on an old mossy log,
Looking very forlorn, sat a little green frog;
He'd a sleek speckled back, and two bright yellow eyes,
And when dining, selected the choicest of flies.

The sun was so hot he scarce opened his eyes,
Far too lazy to stir, let alone watch for flies,
He was nodding, and almost asleep,
When a voice in the branches chirped:
"Froggie, cheep, cheep!"

"You'd better take care," piped the bird to the frog,
"In the water you'll be if you fall off that log.
Can't you see that the streamlet is up to the brim?"
Croaked the froggie: "What odds! You forget I can swim!"

Then the froggie looked up at the bird perched so high
On a bough that to him seemed to reach the sky;
So he croaked to the bird: "If you fall, you will die!"
Chirped the birdie: "What odds! You forget I can fly!"

– Vera Hessey

3 Mysterious Power of Frogs

Serenely poised
The frog sits
And views
The mountain.

– Kikaku

Mainu the Frog

It was Kiman, the son of Kimanze, and he would take a wife. Would he take an earthly maiden? No, he would not. He would take the daughter of Lord Sun and Lady Moon, because once, when she was looking down out of heaven, Kiman had seen her face looking up at him out of a pool, and she was very lovely, white and golden, with the blue of the sky all around her. And since that day he could think of no one else.

So he called Eagle to him, and said, "You, far-flier, will you carry a message to Lord Sun?"

Eagle said, "No, I will not."

Then Kiman called Antelope to him, and said, "You, swift-runner, will you carry a message to Lord Sun?"

Antelope said, "No, I will not."

Then Kiman asked animal after animal, and bird after bird. But none of them would carry his message.

Now he was in despair. He went to sit on the bank of a pond. He said, "Since no one will carry my message, I may as well drown myself."

Then Mainu the Frog scrambled out of the water and said, "You haven't asked *me* to carry your message."

Kiman said, "You! How can *you* get to heaven, when people who have wings cannot?"

Frog said, "I know the way, they do not. Write your message and bring it to me."

So Kiman went home and wrote a letter saying, "I, Kiman, son of Kimanze on earth, I wish to marry the daughter of Lord Sun and Lady Moon." He brought the letter to the pond where Frog was waiting. Frog put the letter in his mouth and hopped away. He hopped, hopped, hopped for a long time. He reached the well where the people of Lord Sun and Lady Moon come down from heaven to fetch water.

And he got into the well and kept quiet.

By and by the girls, the water-carriers, came down from heaven. They came down by a cobweb that Spider had woven. They were carrying empty water jugs. They put the jugs in the well, and Frog got into one of them. The girls filled their jugs; they didn't know that Frog was in one of them. They lifted the full jugs out of the well, and carried them back up the cobweb to heaven. Frog went with them, hidden in the jug.

In a room in the palace of Lord Sun and Lady Moon, the girls, the water-carriers, put down the

jugs on the floor and went away. Frog was swimming round in his jug; now he came out of it. There was a table in the room. Frog jumped on to the table and spat the letter out of his mouth. He left the letter lying on the table, and went to hide in a corner of the room.

By and by in came Lord Sun. He drank some water. He looked on the table, saw the letter. He called the girls, "This letter — who brought it?"

"Master, we don't know." The girls went away.

Lord Sun opens the letter. He reads: "I, Kiman, son of Kimanze on earth, I wish to marry the daughter of Lord Sun and Lady Moon."

Lord Sun thinks, "Kiman, son of Kimanze, is a man that lives on earth. I am a man that lives in heaven. How did this letter come here?" He went away to show the letter to Lady Moon.

Frog stayed in his corner. He stayed many hours. The sky people came and went, taking water from the jugs. And when all the jugs were empty, Frog took a hop and got into one of them.

By and by the girls, the water-carriers, came to fetch the jugs. They went down to earth on the cobweb that Spider had woven. They came to the well, and put the jugs in the water. Frog got out. He stayed at the bottom of the well until the girls had re-filled the jugs and gone back up the cobweb to heaven. Then he went to call on Kiman.

"Kiman, son of Kimanze, I delivered your letter and Lord Sun read it. But he has not yet sent an answer."

Kiman said, "How do I know that you are not telling lies?"

Frog said, "Wait and see."

Kiman waited six days: it seemed like six years. He was stamping with impatience. He wrote another letter: "Lord Sun and Lady Moon, I, Kiman, son of Kimanze, wrote to you, but you did not answer. You did not say, 'We accept you'; you did not say, 'We refuse you.' Say one or the other, that I may know whether I am to live or die."

Kiman gave the letter to Frog. Frog took it in his mouth and went to hide in the well. The girls, the water-carriers, came down from heaven with their jugs. They put the jugs in the water. Frog got into a jug. The girls filled the jugs; they didn't see that Frog was in one of them. They lifted the full jugs out of the well, and went back up the cobweb to heaven.

In a room in the palace of Lord Sun and Lady Moon, the girls, the water-carriers, put down the jugs on the floor and went away. Frog came out of the jug. He jumped on to the table and spat the letter out of his mouth. He left the letter lying on the table, and went to hide in a corner.

By and by in comes Lord Sun. "What, another letter!" He picks it up, reads. He calls the water-carriers. "You girls, since when have you taken to carrying letters about?"

"Master, we have never carried letters."

Lord Sun is troubled. He writes a letter: "Kiman, son of Kimanze, you who send me letters about marrying my daughter. How can I agree before I know you? Come yourself, bringing with you the first-present. When I know you, I can say, 'Yes'."

Lord Sun lays his letter on the table. He goes away. Frog comes out of the corner where he is hiding, climbs up on to the table, takes the letter in his mouth and creeps into an empty water jug. People come and go, taking water from the jugs. When all the jugs are empty, the girls, the water-carriers, come to fetch them. They go with the jugs down to earth by the cobweb Spider has woven.

The girls come to the well, they put the jugs in the water. Frog gets out of his jug and goes to the bottom of the well. The girls, the water-carriers, fill all the jugs and go back up the cobweb to heaven. Frog comes out of the well. It is now night. Frog goes to Kiman's house and knocks on the door: *Flim, flam! Flim, flam!*

Kiman is in bed. He calls, "Who knocks?"

Frog says, "Mainu, the Frog."

Kiman opens the door. Frog gives him the letter. Kiman reads, leaps for joy. He says, "Frog, take what you will from my larder. Sleep anywhere in my house that pleases you. I will go back to my bed. Tomorrow we will decide upon the first-present."

Frog went to Kiman's larder: he didn't like what he found there. But he drank some milk, and he slept where it was cool and pleasant in the draught from the door. In the morning Kiman put forty pearls into a bag. He also wrote a letter.

This is what he wrote: "To you, Lord Sun and Lady Moon, I, Kiman, son of Kimanze, send the first-present. But I myself do not bring it, because I must stay at home to get together the wooing-present. You then send to tell me the amount of the wooing-present, and you shall have it."

Kiman laid the letter on top of the bag that held the pearls and said, "Frog, carry this bag to Lord Sun as a first-present."

Frog said, "My mouth is scarcely big enough to carry it." Kiman said, "You must carry it."

So Frog opened his mouth wide, wide, and stuffed the bag into it. Now he couldn't speak, he could only grunt. He went to the well and hid. The girls, the water-carriers, came down from heaven by the cobweb. They put the jugs in the

water. Frog got into a jug, his jaws were aching; he took the bag out of his mouth and tucked it under his arm.

The girls fill the jugs; they go back up to heaven. In a room in the palace of Lord Sun and Lady Moon they put down the jugs on the floor, and go away. Frog comes out of the jug, jumps on to the table, lays down the bag of pearls and the letter, and goes to hide in a corner of the room.

By and by in come Lord Sun and Lady Moon, walking arm in arm. They drink water. Lord Sun looks on the table. He says, "Again a letter!" He reads the letter, opens the bag, sees the pearls. He says, "Who is it comes with these things? I have never seen him. I don't know his name or what he is like. But he has come a long way; he must be hungry and should be fed."

Lady Moon said, "I will cook a chicken and some sweetcorn and leave it on the table."

Lord Sun said, "Yes, you do that."

They went away. Very soon Lord Sun came back with a letter he had written. The letter says, "Thou, son-in-law, the first-present which thou hast sent me I have received. The amount of the wooing-present which thou shalt give me is a sack of gold."

Lord Sun put the letter on the table and went away.

The time passed. The sky people came and went, fetching water from the jugs until all the jugs were empty. Then in came Lady Moon carrying two dishes: in the one, fried chicken; in the other, sweetcorn. She set the dishes on the table and went away. Frog came out of his corner, jumped on the table. He ate the sweetcorn and left the chicken. He took the letter Lord Sun had written, came down from the table, and jumped into an empty jug. Now he was tired, he fell asleep. He was still sleeping when the girls, the water-carriers, came to fetch the empty jugs. He was still sleeping when they carried the jugs down to earth by the cobweb Spider had woven. He only woke when the girls put the jugs into the well. Then he got out of his jug and hid. The girls filled their jugs and carried them back up the cobweb to heaven. Frog came out of the well and went to Kiman's house.

He knocked: *Flim, flam! Flim, flam!*

"Who knocks?"

"Mainu the Frog."

"Come in."

Frog went in. He gave Kiman Lord Sun's letter.

Kiman read. He rejoiced. He said, "It will take me six days to collect a sack of gold."

Frog said, "And when you have collected it, who is to carry it to heaven?" Kiman said, "You." Frog said, "I cannot carry it. I am not big enough."

Kiman raved and said, "Frog, Frog, will you fail me now? I will not live another day!"

Frog said, "Calm yourself, collect the money. I, Mainu the Frog, am not easily beaten. Give me a piece of gold, and I will find a way of getting the sack to heaven."

Kiman gave Frog a piece of gold, and Frog went away. He went to call on Omari, the medicine man. It took him three days to get to Omari's house. When he got there, he gave Omari the piece of gold, and in return Omari taught Frog two spells: one to make big things small, the other to make small things big. He also taught Frog two ways of breathing: one to make blind, the other to make see again.

Then Frog went back to Kiman and said, "Is the wooing-present, the sack of gold, ready?"

Kiman said, "Yes, it is."

Frog said, "Bring it here."

Kiman brought it. It was forty times as big as Frog. But Frog put his hands on it and said the first spell that Omari had taught him, the spell to make things small. And the sack shrunk till it was no bigger than Frog's thumb.

Kiman was frightened. He cried out, "Oh, oh, all my gold is shrunk away! Now I have nothing to offer to Lord Sun!"

But Frog said, "Stupid! You have plenty to offer. I will show you how much." He said the second spell Omari had taught him, and the sack swelled out to its proper size. Then he said the first spell again, and the sack shrunk. Frog put the sack in his mouth and was hopping away, when Kiman said, "Stop! Stop! You may indeed carry the wooing-present, but who will bring back the bride?"

Frog said, "Have I failed you yet?"

Kiman said, "No."

Frog said, "Neither will I fail you now."

And he went away.

He went to the well. The girls, the water-carriers, came. They filled their jugs, they went back up the cobweb to heaven. They did not know that Frog was in one of the jugs.

The girls set down the jugs in the room of the water. Frog gets out of his jug; he hides in a corner. He waits until Lord Sun and Lady Moon have gone to bed.

Now it is night. All sleep except Frog. Frog comes out of the room of the water. He searches here, searches there; he comes to the room where the daughter of Lord Sun and Lady Moon is sleeping. He hops on to her pillow. He breathes on her eyes. He breathes the first way Omari the medicine man had taught him, the way to make blind. Then he goes back to the room of the water, hides in his corner, and sleeps.

Now comes morning. All the people get up. But the daughter of Lord Sun and Lady Moon does not get up. They say, "What, do you not get up?"

She says, "My eyes are closed, I cannot see." They call Lord Sun and Lady Moon. They come. They say, "What is this? Daughter, open your eyes!" She says, "I cannot! I cannot! I cannot!"

Lord Sun called two messengers. He said, "Take offerings of meat and jewels and go to my wizard, where he sits on his cloud. Ask him the meaning of our daughter's sickness. Ask him also the cure."

The messengers take the offerings of meat and jewels. They set off, they come to where Lord Sun's wizard sits on his cloud. They bow low, they present the offerings, and the wizard says, "What do you wish of me?"

The messengers answer, "The eyes of the daughter of Lord Sun and Lady Moon are shut and will not open. Therefore she cannot see. We would know how to open her eyes that she may see again."

The wizard said, "The maiden is promised in marriage, but not married. The longing of him to whom she is promised has caused this mischief. Let her be given to him, and her eyes will open . . . I have spoken."

The messengers went back to Lord Sun and told the words of the wizard. Lord Sun said, "Very well. But now it is evening. We will all sleep. Tomorrow we will send our daughter down to earth."

Frog had crept close. He heard everything that was said. He went unseen into an empty jug; he was very tired, he slept soundly.

In the morning early, Lord Sun said to Spider,

'Weave a very large cobweb to reach to earth; for, today is the taking down of my daughter to her bridegroom."

So Spider began to weave a new large web. It took him all day. In the meantime, the girls, the water-carriers, took the empty jugs and went down to earth by the old web, and Frog went with them in one of the jugs. The girls came to the well, they put the jugs in the water. Frog came out of the jug in which he was hidden. He stayed at the bottom of the well until the girls had filled all the jugs and gone back up the cobweb to heaven. Then he came up out of the water and went to Kiman's house.

He knocked. *Flim, flam! Flim, flam!* "Kiman, son of Kimanze, open your door. Your bride, the white and golden maiden, daughter of Lord Sun and Lady Moon, today she comes."

"Frog, I fear you are lying. And if you are lying I will have your life!"

"Master, I am truth itself. As for your bride, this evening I will bring her."

Frog went back to the well. He hid. He waited all day. When the sun set Spider finished weaving his new large web. The people of Lord Sun and Lady Moon gathered — a multitude. They came down to earth by the new large web, bringing with them the daughter of Lord Sun and Lady Moon, whose eyes were still closed.

They bore her to the well, they put her down, they left her, and went back up the cobweb. She sits and weeps, seeing nothing. But Frog comes out of the well. He says, "I am Mainu the Frog; I am your guide to him who loves you." He blows, as Omari the medicine man had taught him, the breath that makes the blind see. The maiden's eyes open, she looks round her, she laughs for joy.

Frog said, "Come." And she rose and followed him. He brought her to Kiman's house. They embraced, they married, they were very happy.

And Frog said, "Now there is the joy of one, and the joy of two; the joy of the bride, the joy of the bridegroom. And who brought all this joy to pass? I, Mainu the Frog."

– An Asian Legend

The Frog Barometer

In certain parts of rural Germany, Green Tree Frogs (*Hyla arborea*) were kept in tall, wide-necked bottles, half-filled with soft water into which a miniature wooden ladder was placed. The frogs inevitably climbed towards the top in fine weather and descended at the approach of bad weather. The rungs of the ladder marked the degrees of the barometer, as it were, and travellers consulted the position of the frog before embarking on a trip, believing its sensitivity to be more accurate than any scientific instrument.

Frog Cures

— To get rid of freckles, go to a brook, catch a frog and rub it on the freckles. (U.S.)

— To cure warts rub a live frog over them, then impale it on a thorn to die. (Britain)

— To stop bleeding, bind the cut with linen cloths that had been dipped in "ye green fome where frogges have their spawne 3 days before the new-moon." (17th century, Europe)

— To cure whooping cough, place a small frog in a box tied around the afflicted person's neck. As the frog decays the cough will disappear. (rural England)

— To cure a toothache, spit into a frog's mouth, ask it to carry the ache away, then release it.

— To cure thrush, hold a live frog's head in your mouth. As it breathes it will draw the disease into itself. (Cheshire, England)

— The dried body of a frog worn in a silk bag around the neck will prevent epilepsy and other fits.

— Young frogs swallowed live were a remedy for general weakness, cancer and consumption. (Yorkshire, England)

— To cure rheumatism, roast a live frog and apply it to the sore area. (Utah, U.S.)

Assault

I

I had forgotten how the frogs must sound
After a year of silence, else I think
I should not so have ventured forth alone
At dusk upon this unfrequented road.

II

I am waylaid by Beauty. Who will walk
Between me and the crying of the frogs?
Oh, savage Beauty, suffer me to pass,
That am a timid woman, on her way
From one house to another!

– Edna St. Vincent Millay

What are little boys made of?
What are little boys made of?
Frogs and snails
And puppy-dogs' tails
That's what little boys are made of.

– Nursery Rhyme

And I saw three unclean spirits
like frogs come out of the mouth
of the dragon, and out of the
mouth of the beast, and out of
the mouth of the false prophet.
For they are the spirits of
devils. . . .

– Revelations 16, 13-14, *The Bible*

As it was taught: If there is
dough in a house wherein reptiles
and frogs breed, and pieces are
found in the dough: if they are
mostly reptiles, it is unclean; if
mostly frogs it is clean.

– Kiddushin, *The Babylonian Talmud*

My Aunt Maria asked me to read
the life of Dr. Chalmers, which,
however, I did not promise to do.
Yesterday, Sunday, she was heard
through the partition shouting to
my Aunt Jane, who is deaf,
"Think of it! He stood half an
hour today to hear the frogs
croak, and he wouldn't read the
life of Chalmers."

– Henry David Thoreau

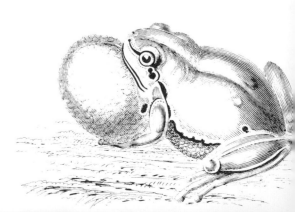

"Ten Thousand Years Goodbye"

in dark.
a great glass tower stands and.

a spiral glass tower stands and.
atop it as if on the verge of vertigo.
a frog.
up on one foot.
gazing at the far side of the universe.

    (o reader join him at that height)

now in the heavens dawn draws near.
eastward sad Nile blue.
ah "Ten Thousand Years, Goodbye!"
musical tadpoles all in staves.
quiet.
quiet.
move.

quiet.
quiet.
moving.

    – Kusano Shimpei

The Frog Prince

In the olden time, when wishing was having, there lived a King, whose daughters were all beautiful; but the youngest was so exceedingly beautiful that the Sun himself, although he saw her very often, was enchanted every time she came out into the sunshine.

Near the castle of this King was a large and gloomy forest, and in the midst stood an old lime-tree, beneath whose branches splashed a little fountain; so, whenever it was very hot, the King's youngest daughter ran off into this wood, and sat down by the side of this fountain; and, when she felt dull, would often divert herself by throwing a golden ball up in the air and catching it. And this was her favourite amusement.

Now, one day it happened, that this golden ball, when the King's daughter threw it into the air, did not fall down into her hand, but on the grass; and then it rolled past her into the fountain. The King's daughter followed the ball with her eyes, but it disappeared beneath the water, which was so deep that no one could see the bottom. Then she began to lament, and to cry louder and louder; and, as she cried, a voice called out, "Why weepest thou, O King's daughter? thy tears would melt even a stone to pity." And she looked around to the spot whence the voice came, and saw a Frog stretching his thick ugly head out of the water. "Ah! you old water-paddler," said she, "was it you that spoke? I am weeping for my golden ball, which has slipped away from me into the water."

"Be quiet, and do not cry," answered the Frog; "I can give thee good advice. But what wilt thou give me if I fetch thy plaything up again?"

"What will you have, dear Frog?" said she. "My dresses, my pearls and jewels, or the golden crown which I wear?"

The Frog answered, "Dresses, or jewels, or golden crowns, are not for me; but if thou wilt love me, and let me be thy companion and playfellow, and sit at thy table, and eat from thy little golden plate, and drink out of thy cup, and sleep in thy little bed, — if thou wilt promise me all these, then will I dive down and fetch up thy golden ball."

"Oh, I will promise you all," said she, "if you will only get me my ball." But she thought to herself, "What is the silly Frog chattering about? Let him remain in the water with his equals; he cannot mix in society." But the Frog, as soon as he had received her promise, drew his head under the water and dived down. Presently he swam up again with the ball in his mouth, and threw it on the grass. The King's daughter was full of joy when she again saw her beautiful plaything; and, taking it up, she ran off immediately. "Stop! stop!" cried the Frog; "take me with thee. I cannot run as thou canst." But all his croaking was useless; although it was loud enough, the King's daughter did not hear it, but, hastening home, soon forgot the poor Frog, who was obliged to leap back into the fountain.

The next day, when the King's daughter was sitting at table with her father and all his courtiers, and was eating from her own little golden plate, something was heard coming up the marble stairs, splish-splash, splish-splash; and when it arrived at the top, it knocked at the door, and a voice said, "Open the door, thou youngest daughter of the King!" So she rose and went to see who it was that called her; but when she opened the door and caught sight of the Frog, she shut it again with great vehemence, and sat down at the table, looking very pale. But the King perceived that her heart was beating violently, and asked her whether it was a giant who had come to fetch her away who stood at the door. "Oh, no!" answered she; "it was no giant, but an ugly Frog."

"What does the Frog want with you?" said the King.

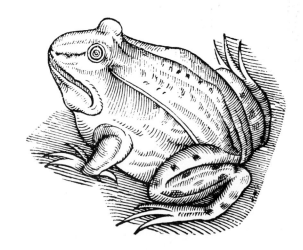

"Oh, dear father, when I was sitting yesterday playing by the fountain, my golden ball fell into the water, and this Frog fetched it up again because I cried so much: but first, I must tell you, he pressed me so much, that I promised him he should be my companion. I never thought that he could come out of the water, but somehow he has jumped out, and now he wants to come in here."

At that moment there was another knock, and a voice said,

King's daughter, youngest,
Open the door.
Hast thou forgotten
Thy promise made
At the fountain so clear
'Neath the lime-tree's shade?
King's daughter, youngest,
Open the door.

Then the King said, "What you have promised, that you must perform; go and let him in." So the King's daughter went and opened the door, and the Frog hopped in after her right up to her chair: and as soon as she was seated, the Frog said, "Take me up"; but she hesitated so long that at last the King ordered her to obey. And as soon as the Frog sat on the chair, he jumped on to the table, and said, "Now push thy plate near me, that we may eat together." And she did so, but as everyone saw, very unwillingly. The Frog seemed to relish his dinner much, but every bite that the King's daughter ate nearly choked her, till at last the Frog said, "I have satisfied my hunger and feel very tired; wilt thou carry me upstairs now into thy chamber, and make thy bed ready that we may sleep together?" At this speech the King's daughter began to cry, for she was afraid of the cold Frog, and dared not touch him; and besides, he actually wanted to sleep in her own beautiful, clean bed.

But her tears only made the King very angry, and he said, "He who helped you in the time of your trouble, must not now be despised!" So she took the Frog up with two fingers, and put him in a corner of her chamber. But as she lay in her bed, he crept up to it, and said, "I am so very tired that I shall sleep well; do take me up or I will tell thy father." This speech put the King's daughter in a terrible passion, and catching the Frog up, she threw him with all her strength against the wall, saying, "Now, will you be quiet, you ugly Frog?"

But as he fell he was changed from a frog into a handsome Prince with beautiful eyes, who, after a little while became, with her father's consent, her dear companion and betrothed. Then he told her how he had been transformed by an evil witch, and that no one but herself could have had the power to take him out of the fountain; and that on the morrow they would go together into his own kingdom.

The next morning, as soon as the sun rose, a carriage drawn by eight white horses, with ostrich feathers on their heads, and golden bridles, drove up to the door of the palace, and behind the carriage stood the trusty Henry, the servant of the young Prince. When his master was changed into a frog, trusty Henry had grieved so much that he had bound three iron bands round his heart, for fear it should break with grief and sorrow. But now that the carriage was ready to carry the young Prince to his own country, the faithful Henry helped in the bride and bridegroom, and placed himself in the seat behind, full of joy at his master's release. They had not proceeded far when the Prince heard a crack as if something had broken behind the carriage; so he put his head out of the window and asked Henry what was broken, and Henry answered, "It was not the carriage, my master, but a band which I bound round my heart when it was in such grief because you were changed into a frog."

Twice afterwards on the journey there was the same noise, and each time the Prince thought that it was some part of the carriage that had given away; but it was only the breaking of the bands which bound the heart of the trusty Henry, who was thenceforward free and happy.

– A Version of the Traditional Fairy Tale, by Lucy Crane, 1875

4 Trials and Tribulations of Frogs

Bending over
The frog's grave,
A deutzia tree drops
Pure white tears.

– Issa

Across the Andes by Frog

In 1971 a plucky Dane, Knud Svenson, became the first man to attempt to cross the Andes by frog. The expedition was to start in Iquique, capital of North Chile, and traverse 500 miles through the thickest part of the Andes to Santa Cruz in Bolivia — see map attached. Svenson had already attempted (and failed) to sail round the world on a rabbit and his attempt to cross Spitzbergen on a halibut had proved spectacularly unsuccessful in 1958. What follows is Svenson's personal account of one of the most arduous journeys ever attempted, across the Andes by frog.

Iquique: Jan 19th: Expedition delayed by three days after the frog was squashed when I sat on it. We wait around in the sultry heat of this coastal town whilst another frog is found.

Iquique: Jan 21st: A perfect day to set off. The sunshine was bright, but a strongish north-easterly wind kept us cool. The baggage porters had at last settled their differences over pay, and the forecast was good. However as soon as I mounted the frog I squashed it again. Oh, the frustrations! We must reach the Andean foothills by mid-February, or the vicious South American winter will set in.

Iquique: Jan 26th: I have tried mounting frogs without a saddle and even tried with my haversack off, but they always squash as soon as I sit down on them. Have decided to try a different approach. I will walk and the frog can carry the baggage. It will be hard work especially in the mountains, but I would rather suffer some discomfort than give up now.

Iquique: Jan 27th: The frog has proved incapable of carrying even the lightest hold-all. Seven or eight were squashed last night, while we were trying to load up.

Iquique: Jan 28th: Today, at last, we set out from the main square here in Iquique, on the 500-mile journey to Santa Cruz in Bolivia. The frog, unladen by any baggage, set a furious pace, and we lost it through a hole in the wall not ten yards from where we started.

Iquique: Feb 6th: The days pass by in a long frustrating week, whilst we design a special frog harness. The Andean winter gets closer as every day goes by.

Iquique: Feb 7th: The frogs are so slippery any harness is almost impossible to fit. They are sending to Belgium for a specialist.

Iquique: March 30th: At last the Belgian specialist has arrived. He says that frogs are totally unsuitable for this sort of journey. The man is a complete fraud. We refuse to pay his return fare.

Iquique: March 31st: Wake up with a huge Malaysian Leper Frog at my throat. The Belgian specialist eventually calls it off, after we promise to pay his fare back.

Iquique: March 32nd: Decide to set off with frog in a box. The weather holds out, and we make good progress. We reach the outskirts of Pozo Almonte before I discover someone has let the frog out of the box.

Pozo Almonte: March 33rd: I am beginning to have suspicions about my Chilean calendar.

Pozo Almonte: March 34th: Success! I discover a frog in my lunch, so I put him in the box and set out again.

Iquique: March 35th: I must have misread the map. Bump into the Belgian specialist in the street. Hits me with a South American Singing Toad, which he was taking to the vet. I report him to the RSPCA.

Iquique: March 36th: RSPCA man arrived from London. He says he has called about a matter of sixteen frogs squashed while under my care.

Heathrow Airport: March 37th: It appears that the Andes are too steep and mountainous to be really suitable for crossing by frog. Perhaps I should start on something smaller. Decide to attempt the first crossing of the Skagerrak by maggot.

March 43rd: Decide to throw away my calendar.

– Bert Fegg's Nasty Book For Boys and Girls

The Frog and the Crow

There was a jolly frog in the river did swim, O!
And a comely black crow lived by the river brim, O!

    Come on shore, come on shore,
    Said the crow to the frog, and then, O!
    No, you'll bite me, no, you'll bite me,
    Said the frog to the crow again, O!

But there is sweet music on yonder green hill, O!
And you'll be a dancer, a dancer in yellow,

    All in yellow, all in yellow,
    Said the crow to the frog, and then, O!
    All in yellow, all in yellow,
    Said the frog to the crow again, O!

Farewell, ye little fishes, farewell every good fellow,
For I'm going to be a dancer, a dancer in yellow.

    Oh beware, take care,
    Said the fish to the frog, and then, O!
    All in yellow, all in yellow,
    Said the frog to the fish again, O!

The frog he came swimming, a-swimming to land, O!
The crow he came hopping to lend a hand, O!

    Sir, I thank you, sir, I thank you,
    Said the frog to the crow, and then, O!
    You are welcome, most welcome,
    Said the crow to the frog again, O!

But where is the music on yonder green hill, O?
And where are the dancers, the dancers in yellow?

    All in yellow, all in yellow,
    Said the frog to the crow again, O!
    They are here, said the crow,
    And ate him up there and then, O!

– Anonymous

A Strange Frog Ceremony

In the neighbourhood of Pilsen (Bohemia) a conical hut of green branches, without any door, is erected at Whitsuntide in the midst of the village. To this hut rides a troop of village lads with a king at their head . . . . In his train are a judge, a crier, and a personage called the Frog-flayer or Hangman. This last is a sort of ragged merryandrew, wearing a rusty old sword and bestriding a sorry hack. . . . When (the first part of the ceremony) is over, the Frog-flayer steps forward and, after exhibiting a cage with frogs in it, sets up a gallows on which he hangs the frogs in a row. In the neighbourhood of Plas the ceremony differs in some points. . . . When the village dames and girls are being criticised at the arbour, a frog is secretly pinched and poked by the crier till it quacks. Sentence of death is passed on the frog by the king; the hangman beheads it and flings the bleeding body among the spectators.

– Sir James George Frazier, *The Golden Bough*

The Frog Race

At the ammunition depot there was a small, muddy, permanent detachment of Ordnance Corps soldiers, swelled each night by the twenty men from the other inland units. One of the Ordnance men was a corporal who used to organise bullfrog races for money.

The men who were at the depot all the time, and had very little to do except see that it did not blow up and was not stolen, had their own private bullfrogs which they painted different colours and kept in boxes. They trained them to race and initiated the actual races by flaring a small dash of gunpowder a couple of yards behind them. The races were held along a wide curving concrete gully that ran the length of the depot. It was supposed to be full of water for use if the ammunition caught fire, but the soldiers regularly drained the water away so that they could hold the races. The depot was always sticky with mud and engineers were always searching for a leak or a fault in the gully.

On most nights the bets on the events were small, but on pay nights the stakes would pile. The men who had arrived to guard for a single night had to go and catch their own bullfrogs in the clammy undergrowth, but it was not difficult because there were hundreds of them and they made a lot of noise.

But these wild frogs were mostly no threat to the trained frogs. They were given a stripe or two of distinguishing paint, but they rarely reacted to the sizzling of the small pile of gunpowder in the way that the experienced ones did. There were no odds given, only in side bets, the rule being the stake in the kitty and the winner take all.

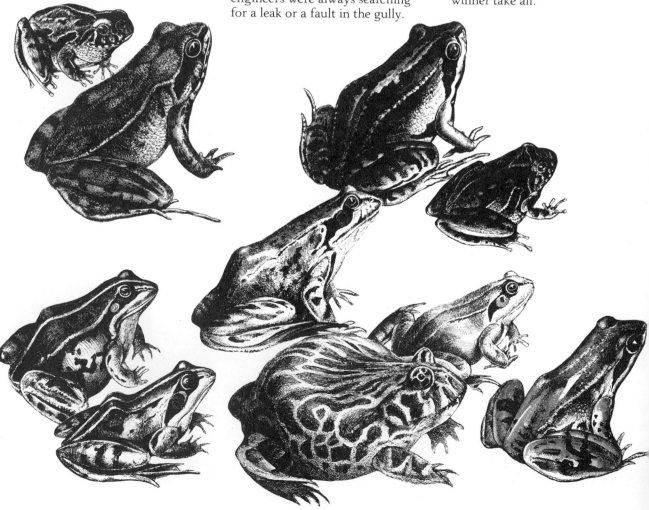

Brigg had never had a frog because he had no money to put on its back. But the Ordnance man said that since he was there so frequently he ought to get himself one and train it.

He first saw his frog posturing in a patch of cream moonlight. It was the early-hour patrol, when the jungle all around was all screams and whispers. Brigg walked the perimeter path of the depot, the wires of his nerves bending at every swift sound. No matter how many times he did the duty his reactions never softened.

The bullfrog was singing throatily in the middle of the path. It was a bulky and strong-looking frog, but not too fat: the sort that could do well in the longer races. He was facing Brigg, quite impudently, his jelly eyes protruding from his flat black head, and his pale waistcoat thumping and sobbing with the emotion of his elegy.

When Brigg had made up his mind to catch him, and had moved towards him, the frog bounded half-left, flopping on the dead leaves at the fringe of the path. It was a good jump for sideways and Brigg knew by now that the front jump was always half as powerful again.

"Here, boy," encouraged Brigg, slinking towards him. "Come on. Good frog."

The creature gave a short, low leap, and then another. His glowing belly tickled against the leaves as he went.

"Good, that was good," Brigg told him. "You could be a champ, son. Come on, come here."

The frog spat at him as he went towards it again. He was a fighter too. That was even better. Brigg rushed him and he went heaving along towards the darker places under the trees. Going after him, Brigg knew that if he was ever going to have a frog to race for him it would have to be this one. The animal seemed bent on proving Brigg's choice, because he jumped at right angles again and tumbled into the wide, hard gully where they held the races.

"Now let's see," whispered Brigg with soft delight. "Now we'll see how you go." He chased the bullfrog in an unhurried way, going forward demonstratively every time the thing landed after a leap, thus forcing it into another immediately. They followed the bends and straights of the long gully through well over half its distance. Then the frog sat down still and tame and allowed Brigg to fold it in his beret.

He took it to the guardroom and put it in the empty tea bucket until morning. The tea bucket had a lid to keep the tea warm, so the frog could not escape. He took it out again before the dawn guard went off for the tea.

The Ordnance soldiers thought the frog was a promising one. They agreed to look after it when Brigg was not doing a guard duty and they gave it a big ammunition box, plenty of mud and leaves and some spiders to eat. Brigg chose yellow and white as his racing colours and he painted stripes of these down his frog's back. When he went back to Panglin he sold his camera for twenty dollars and went back on guard at the ammunition depot on the next pay day.

As soon as the duty officer had circled on his inspection tour at ten o'clock that night, the racing started. Nearly all the temporary guards had caught frogs and had money with which to back them.

Brigg collected his frog and inspected it. It seemed a bit thinner than when he had captured it, but this was good.

"You'll have to call it something," said the Corporal who organised the racing. "What's it going to be?"

"Lucy," said Brigg suddenly. "Juicy Lucy."

"You can't call a bullfrog Lucy," said the Corporal doubtfully. "Can you?"

"I am," said Brigg.

"All right," said the Corporal. "It's a mare then."

"No, it's a girl," said Brigg, and the Corporal looked at him oddly.

The first race was a short one over twenty feet, for dollar stakes. Some of the soldiers did not enter their frogs but stood watching by the white sugar light of the depot's flood lamps which had been diverted from the ammunition dumps to the race-track. They cosseted their frogs in their hats or in boxes, or the ammunition pouches attached to their webbing belts. Some of the frogs made a loud and unhappy noise, but those in the ammunition pouches mostly coughed because of the smell and dust of the blanco.

A muslin net from the cookhouse was used to hold the racers immediately before the start as the powder, emptied from a .303 cartridge, was approached by the small flame biting its way along the short fuse. It sizzled, giving off small explosions, always sharp but not too loud, and the officer in command was dependably in the distant mess by this time. Some of the officers knew about the racing and sometimes turned up to watch. But they only had side bets on other people's frogs because they had none of their own.

Brigg put his frog under the net with the others. The spiteful little flame nibbled down the fuse. When the net was adeptly pulled away just before the big flare-up Brigg's frog was facing the wrong way. He shouted at it. But the gunpowder flamed and the creatures went hopping off crazily. Brigg's frog jumped sideways and straddled the warted back of one of the other entrants so that both were immediately without a hope in the race.

It was a two-dollar race next. Brigg doubtfully dropped his money into the stake-keeper's greasy beret. His frog was throbbing in the cup of his hand, staring out with a blank, unbelieving ogle, and croaking as though its heart was breaking.

"This time, Lucy," said Brigg quietly, "face the right bleeding way. And jump. Understand? Jump."

There were more entrants this time. Twelve, fat, uncertain, protesting things, stuffed under the muslin net and giving leaps and groaning jumps beneath it so that it bulged and sagged and quivered as though it were alive itself. Brigg put his frog quite surely facing the right way and joined his anxious face to the ring of lit, concerned, faces around the gully. The charge burned and fanned noisily and away the frogs flew. Sometimes some leapt clear of the gully, and the owners, following wildly along the bank were permitted under the rules to throw them back into the race, but one pace back from the place where they had left the course.

Almost stifled with excitement, Brigg saw his frog leap gracefully into the lead from the start. It went in gliding, bounding arcs, landing straight and confident and seeming to know where it was going and what was expected of it. The race was over fifty feet and Lucy had a ten-length lead when the first and only bend was gained. Brigg ran with the others, slipping and scrambling along the bank, running all of them, with a funny crippled, bending run, their faces down low near their frogs, mouthing curses and encouragement, urging, stumbling and sometimes falling over.

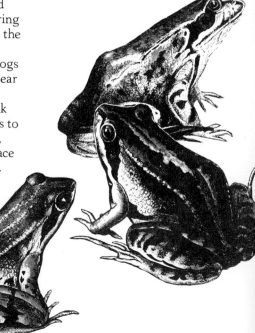

When Brigg's frog was clear of the bend, it sat down. It seemed happy and satisfied with its performance and took on a frozen immobility that none of Brigg's shrieking altered by even a jerk of a muscle.

"Move, you black bastard!" howled Brigg almost on his knees with involuntary pleading and the need to get as near to his animal's ears as he could. But Lucy sat blandly and blindly and allowed the rest of the field to pass. Just as the winning frog crossed the final line in mid-leap, Lucy came alive again and executed a small token leap. Then she sat, full of her private thoughts again, until the stewards announced that the race was run and won and Brigg stepped down to pick her up. Then she really jumped, clean through his pincher arms and down the straight course like a thoroughbred. Brigg ran in pursuit, a hundred feet along the gully and then out into the wet and heavy going of the perimeter road and its collar of bush and brush.

"I'll catch you, you bugger," promised Brigg as he ran, sliding down banks, caught by the fingernails of thorny creepers strung from the thicker trees. One of the entrails cut him across the face like a lash, filling his eyes with water and bringing a taste of blood to his mouth. But he never lost the bullfrog. It was always just ahead, sometimes bounding, sometimes slithering, sometimes impudently resting, waiting for him to catch up. Then it surrendered, again without fuss,

sitting squatly on a flat leaf and waiting for Brigg to reach and pick it up.

He carried it back. If it had not escaped he might have abandoned it as a racing frog and saved his scarce money. But now he was decided to try once more. Just once. He left it out of the next two races, watching instead the silent capers of the frogs and the rowdy antics of the owners.

The last race was for a ten-dollar stake per man. There were twenty frogs entered. Brigg put his money into the hat with a sad shrug, and placed the curiously dry-wet belly of the frog on the starting area. It was a crowded start, with frogs climbing on other frogs' backs, investigating other frogs' ears and smells, and all finally smothered by the wide white net, held down firmly at each corner by the hands of the stewards.

It was over seventy-five feet around two bends and into a short, straight finish. The strong impersonal floodlights glared down on the grouped soldiers in green, hunched and anxious, waiting for the start.

The gunpowder charge spluttered and suddenly spread and the taut faces flowed into mobility, working and shouting and urging as the frogs launched themselves away from the sudden sound.

Lucy went off like rubber, throwing herself forward from bound to bound and immediately into the first three, the yellow and white stripes on her back wrinkling and stretching like elastic with each free and muscled movement. Because the start was so crowded several frogs were left sprawling in the mud at the line, two were stonily facing the opposite way from the course and one had a seizure and died immediately the starting charge went off.

Others leapt on to the sides of the gully, out of the ruck and rush, only to be flung back into the race by angry owners. On either side of the gully the soldiers ran hysterically, willing on the slimy racers, their faces transformed by the bright, holy, hopeful light that shines on those consumed by greed and gambling.

Brigg loped along one side of the gully, praying that Lucy would not jump out of the race on the other side. This had finished the chances of several owners who lost every thread of hope in the time it took to run around the gully to reach their stupid champions. Some soldiers threw the frogs forlornly into the fray again, one or two patted them with understanding, put them in their pockets for another night or sent them on their way into the undergrowth. Others threw the frogs aside in hate and disgust and one flung his entrant high and murderously at the shining moon.

After thirty feet there were eight racers left of the twenty. Lucy was contesting the front with a vicious bull who jumped as though he had been promised freedom if he won. Brigg had stopped shouting now, his breath too meagre to form words let alone bawl them. The big bull belonged to a sparse-haired lance-corporal going like an ape along the opposite bank, calling to it in thick Liverpool phrases. The frog had a white skull and crossbones on its broad pimpled back.

Third was a little beetle of a frog, bearing a red cross like some undernourished Crusader, busily making ground a few inches behind the squared backsides of the two in front. This one was running for a Medical Corps corporal who had shot it with dope behind a secret tree two minutes before the start.

Lucy was a snout ahead at each skimming jump. She was using her low-leap technique, taking off like a hare instead of a frog, barely leaving the ground, but economising on effort with every jump. The big bull was taking a breath at each landing, but every time he pushed out with his steely springers he went in a high parabola, long and powerful, but still not quite matching the neat, straight jumps of Lucy.

At the second bend Lucy stopped, squatted squarely, and emitted a loud honk, a sound loaded with satisfaction. Brigg covered his face with his fingers. He tried to shout, but the words came out noiselessly, like jugged air.

"Please," he eventually framed. "Please, for Jesus' sake. Please, frog."

No reaction came from Lucy. The big skull-and-crossbones bull was bounding ahead and the stimulated beetle-frog with the red cross flew by on a wave of hypertension. Others followed and passed.

Tragedy seemed complete for Brigg when Lucy suddenly skimmed forward again, as though she had merely been collecting her breath. But the beetle-frog, at almost the same instant, flopped into the mud and died. As Brigg was urging his frog again into the contest, the big bull belonging to the Liverpool soldier stopped and began groaning and thumping rhythmically two feet from the finishing line.

Its owner cried bleakly and rolled and postulated on the side of the gully begging, threatening and willing his frog to finish the race. The frog stared a deep liquid stare, straight ahead.

Lucy went through the field like a charger. She leapt on joyously with Brigg at her side. He shouted nothing now, just made little sounds with his mouth and sweated and stumbled as he ambled. She went by the dead beetle-frog and overtook some of the hopefuls who had gone by when she was resting. Then, when she was level with the skull-and-crossbones frog, she came to another sudden stop and squatted again, completely level with her rival, eight inches to his left. They sat, intent, like two old women watching a love film. The Liverpool youth looked over the gully at Brigg, an uncertain triumph rolling over his face. Brigg looked at him, then got down and began to hiss at Lucy, low spurts of breath that he hoped sounded like a snake.

Both frogs remained motionless perhaps in some secret communication. The stragglers were catching up now. A ghastly red-painted animal was puffing its way up the track in the lead of three others.

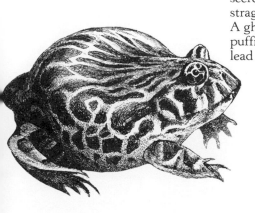

Then the big bull jumped three inches and his owner sprang with excitement against the sky. Lucy seemed to consider the move, leapt four inches then another three and finally made a smart and graceful jump across the finishing line.

Brigg shouted and stamped. He leaned over, laughing, and caught his frog in the tender bed of his hands.

"Oh, you beauty," he giggled. "Oh, you bloody beauty."

He saw the Liverpool soldier try to crack his frog like a nut with the sole of his boot. But it moved faster than at any time in the race. He made another murderous attempt and missed again. The frog bounded away like a ball.

Brigg collected his two hundred dollars. He took Lucy to a far part of the depot, kissed her thick, damp head and released her to her native country.

The next day he put in for some leave.

– Leslie Thomas, *The Virgin Soldiers*

Advertising Frogs

Trade cards from the past
exploiting frogs for commercial
purposes.

Thus use your frog: put your
hook through his mouth and out
at his gills, and then with a fine
needle and silk sew the upper
part of his leg with only one
stitch to the arming wire of your
hook, or tie the frog's leg above
the upper joint to the armed wire;
and in so doing use him as
though you loved him.

– Izaak Walton, *The Compleat Angler*

It was the saying of Bion, that though boys throw stones at frogs in sport, yet the frogs do not die in sport but in earnest.

– Plutarch

I'll risk forty dollars that he can outjump any frog in Calaveros County. I don't see no points about that frog that's any better than any other frog.

– Mark Twain, *The Celebrated Jumping Frog*

Frog in Your Throat?

The public is warned against all bronchial lozenges which imitate Frog in Your Throat in shape, color, trade-mark and trade dress. All such imitations will be suppressed by process of law. None genuine unless stamped with the word frog.

If frogs, which are not commanded concerning the sanctification of the Divine Name, yet it is written of them, and they shall come up and go into thy house . . . and into thine ovens, and into thy kneading troughs.

– Pesahim, *The Babylonian Talmud*

Well, I woke up in the morning
There's frogs inside my socks

– Bob Dylan, *On The Road Again*

Scientific Frogs

"We will have yet more terrible things to endure"

The prophetic cry of the choir of frogs in Aristophanes' play of 405 B.C. has been richly fulfilled. Frogs have been the subject of more laboratory investigations than any other living creatures. Their anatomy has been studied and described more fully than that of any animal except man. Unfortunately for frogs, they possess several qualities that lead to their ultimate dissection. They are readily accessible, easily caught and simple to keep in captivity. But it is their remarkable capacity for surviving experimental operations that has endeared them to scientists, and made them suitable for many demonstrations and investigations where shock, loss of blood and infection would lay a lesser creature low. However scientific frogs have not all croaked in vain. Many important discoveries have been made with the help of the frog and prompted people like Carl Jung to pay thoughtful tribute to them: "Given its anatomy, the frog, more than any of the cold-blooded animals, anticipates Man."

Probing their miracles and natural secrets

"I would on first setting out, inform the reader that there is a much greater number of miracles and natural secrets in the frog than anyone hath ever before thought of or discovered."

Thus spoke Jan Swammerdam, a Dutch physician, naturalist and microscopist. Jan and his physiological predecessors armed with knives and scalpels have been hacking away at frogs in the name of science for 350 years.

The English physician William Harvey began filleting frogs in 1628 because "motions of the heart are more obvious in the colder animals." His martyred amphibians were commemorated in *The Anatomical Dissertation Concerning the Motion of the Heart and Blood in Animals*, the publication generally agreed to mark the beginning of the scientific study of biology.

With the aid of many beating frog hearts Harvey set forth his theory that blood follows a continuous circuit, flowing away from the heart in the arteries and towards it in the veins.

Then came Swammerdam who carved a swath through the liver and lungs into the most intimate regions of his frogs. Hunched over a microscope he spent months exploring the genitals of the male frog and the ovaries of impregnated females. His detailed drawings published in 1737 include instructions for finding the eggs dispersed in a frog's belly somewhere in their passage through the tube into the uterus.

The pleasures of dissected tadpoles

These early investigations into the sexual apparatus of frogs were continued by another Dutch microscopist and anatomist, one Anton van Leeuwenhoek. His exhaustive analysis of reproductive organs and squirming spermatozoa led him, naturally enough, to tadpoles which he proceeded to chop to pieces. Amidst the remains of the would-be frog under his microscope Anton found entertainment. Observing the capillaries in the gills of the tadpole he wrote " . . . I saw to my great amusement very clearly the circulation of the blood,

which was pushed along from the parts nearest to the body to those farthest away from it." The closer he looked the more thrilling it became until. . . "The motion of the blood in these tadpoles exceeds all the small animals and fish I have seen; nay, this pleasure has often-times been so recreating to me, that I do not believe that all the pleasure of fountains or waterworks, either natural or made by art, could have pleased my sight so well, as the view of these creatures have given me."

Frogs' legs and lightning bolts

On his way to contributing the word galvanize to the dictionary and inventing the electric battery, Luigi Galvani was ably assisted by the legs of a frog which he hitched to a lightning bolt. It all

began innocently enough in the laboratory of this Italian physician one day in 1768. . . "I had dissected and prepared a frog, and while I was attending to something else, I laid it on a table on which stood an electrical machine at some distance. . . Now when one of the persons who were present touched accidently and lightly the inner crural nerves of the frog with the point of a scalpel all the muscles of the legs seemed to contract again and again. Another who was there thought that he had noticed that the action was excited when a spark was discharged from the conductor of the machine. Whereupon I was inflamed with an incredible zeal and eagerness to test the same and to bring to light what was concealed in it."

Luigi's zeal and eagerness took him up onto the roof of his house where, taking advantage of a convenient thunderstorm, he tied a wire to a metallic conductor. The other end of the wire was fastened to the frog and — Eureka! "As often as the lightning broke forth, the muscles were thrown into repeated violent convulsions, so that always, as the lightning lightened the sky, the muscle contractions and movements preceded the thunder and, as it were, announced its coming."

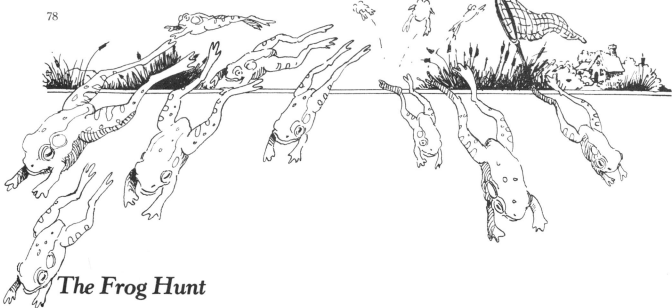

The Frog Hunt

The frog pool was square — fifty feet wide and seventy feet long and four feet deep. Lush soft grass grew about its edge and a little ditch brought the water from the river to it and from it little ditches went out to the orchards. There were frogs there all right, thousands of them. Their voices beat the night, they boomed and barked and croaked and rattled. They sang to the stars, to the waning moon, to the waving grasses. They bellowed love songs and challenges. The men crept through the darkness toward the pool. The captain carried a nearly filled pitcher of whisky and every man had his own glass. The captain had found them flashlights that worked. Hughie and Jones carried gunny sacks. As they drew quietly near, the frogs heard them coming. The night had been roaring with frog song and then suddenly it was silent. Mack and the boys and the captain sat down on the ground to have one last short one and to map their campaign. And the plan was bold.

During the millennia that frogs and men have lived in the same world, it is probable that men have hunted frogs. And during that time a pattern of hunt and parry has developed. The man with net or bow or lance or gun creeps noiselessly, as he thinks, toward the frog. The pattern requires that the frog sit still, sit very still and wait. The rules of the game require the frog to wait until the final flicker of a second, when the net is descending, when the lance is in the air, when the finger squeezes the trigger, then the frog jumps, plops into the water, swims to the bottom and waits until the man goes away. That is the way it is done, the way it has always been done. Frogs have every right to expect it will always be done that way. Now and then the net is too quick, the lance pierces, the gun flicks and that frog is gone, but it is all fair and in the framework. Frogs don't resent that. But how could they have anticipated Mack's new method? How could they have foreseen the horror that followed? The sudden flashing of lights, the shouting and squealing of men, the rush of feet. Every frog leaped, plopped into the pool, and swam frantically to the bottom. Then into the pool plunged the line of men, stamping, churning, moving in a crazy line up the pool, flinging their feet about. Hysterically the frogs displaced from their placid spots swam ahead of the crazy thrashing feet and the feet came on. Frogs are good swimmers but they haven't much endurance. Down the pool they went until finally they were bunched and crowded against the end. And the feet and wildly plunging bodies followed them. A few frogs lost their heads and floundered among the feet and got through and these were saved. But the majority decided to leave this pool forever, to find a new home in a new country where this kind of thing didn't happen. A wave of frantic, frustrated frogs, big ones, little ones, brown ones, green ones, men frogs and women frogs, a wave of them broke over the bank, crawled, leaped, scrambled. They clambered up the grass, they clutched at each other, little ones rode on big ones. And then — horror on horror — the flashlights found them. Two men gathered them like berries. The line came out of the water and closed in on their rear and gathered them like potatoes. Tens and fifties of them were flung into the gunny sacks, and the sacks filled with tired, frightened, and disillusioned frogs, with dripping, whimpering frogs. Some got away, of course, and some had been saved in the pool. But never in frog history had such an execution taken place. Frogs by the pound, by the fifty pounds. They weren't counted but there must have been six or seven hundred. Then happily Mack tied up the necks of the sacks. They were soaking, dripping wet and the air was cool. They had a short one in the grass before they went back to the house so they wouldn't catch cold.

— John Steinbeck, *Cannery Row*

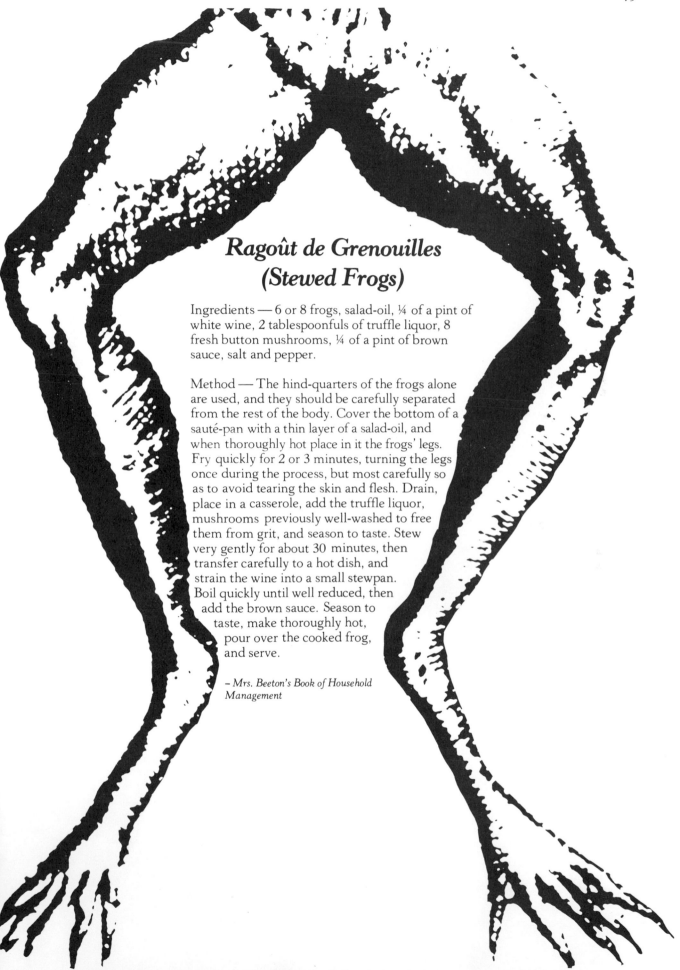

Ragoût de Grenouilles
(Stewed Frogs)

Ingredients — 6 or 8 frogs, salad-oil, ¼ of a pint of white wine, 2 tablespoonfuls of truffle liquor, 8 fresh button mushrooms, ¼ of a pint of brown sauce, salt and pepper.

Method — The hind-quarters of the frogs alone are used, and they should be carefully separated from the rest of the body. Cover the bottom of a sauté-pan with a thin layer of a salad-oil, and when thoroughly hot place in it the frogs' legs. Fry quickly for 2 or 3 minutes, turning the legs once during the process, but most carefully so as to avoid tearing the skin and flesh. Drain, place in a casserole, add the truffle liquor, mushrooms previously well-washed to free them from grit, and season to taste. Stew very gently for about 30 minutes, then transfer carefully to a hot dish, and strain the wine into a small stewpan. Boil quickly until well reduced, then add the brown sauce. Season to taste, make thoroughly hot, pour over the cooked frog, and serve.

– *Mrs. Beeton's Book of Household Management*

5 Strange Encounters with Frogs

A giant frog and I
Glare at each other
Sitting face to face
In silence.

– Issa

Calamitous Frogs

1. And the Lord spake unto Moses, Go unto Pharaoh, and say unto him, Thus saith the Lord, Let my people go, that they may serve me.

2. And if thou refuse to let them go, behold, I will smite all thy borders with frogs:

3. And the river shall bring forth frogs abundantly, which shall go up and come into thine house, and into thy bedchamber, and upon thy bed, and into the house of thy servants, and upon thy people, and into thine ovens, and into thy kneadingtroughs:

4. And the frogs shall come up both on thee, and upon thy people, and upon all thy servants.

5. And the Lord spake unto Moses, Say unto Aaron, Stretch forth thine hand with thy rod over the streams, over the rivers, and over the ponds, and cause frogs to come up upon the land of Egypt.

6. And Aaron stretched out his hand over the waters of Egypt; and the frogs came up, and covered the land of Egypt.

7. And the magicians did so with their enchantments, and brought up frogs upon the land of Egypt.

8. Then Pharaoh called for Moses and Aaron, and said, Intreat the Lord, that he may take away the frogs from me, and from my people; and I will let the people go, that they may do sacrifice unto the Lord.

9. And Moses said unto Pharaoh, Glory over me: when shall I intreat for thee, and for thy servants, and for thy people, to destroy the frogs from thee and thy houses, that they may remain in the river only?

10. And he said, To morrow. And he said, Be it according to thy word: that thou mayest know that there is none like unto the Lord our God.

11. And the frogs shall depart from thee, and from thy houses, and from thy servants, and from thy people; they shall remain in the river only.

12. And Moses and Aaron went out from Pharaoh: and Moses cried unto the Lord because of the frogs which he had brought against Pharaoh.

13. And the Lord did according to the word of Moses; and the frogs died out of the houses, out of the villages, and out of the fields.

14. And they gathered them together upon heaps: and the land stank.

– Exodus, Chapter 8 of *The Bible*

The Frog Plague

In stagnant pools, by disused tennis-courts,
Time breeds us mediocre monsters
To reproach us for our gross indifference. . .
Tadpoles bud with slick perversity
Into swart hoppers who at once assume
Proprietorial airs that would be comic
Were it not for their capacity to proliferate
And swarm across the flagstones and with grave
Deliberation mate on patios
In full view of a score of distinguished guests.
Drains become blocked, water-tanks fouled while cisterns
Afford a means of ingress for their tribe;
The nights are soggy with their coarse *bavarde*.
Their spawn like dirty sago clots the lake,
And where the swan-limbed younger-set once swam
The water ripples idly in the wake
Of bulb-eyed shagreen parvenu frog-kicking
With all the leisure of the permanent resident.

It makes small difference how our fears are rendered
Sufferable by sadism, by frog-hunts
At week-end parties with gilt trophies for
The biggest bag, the biggest single bull,
Nor how we seek to wed utility
To murder by creating false demands
For frog-skin gloves and purses or a taste
For haunches *à la casserole* — beyond
The temporary regimen of the hedge,
Beyond the nervous lamp-light and the men
Standing around the rooms as if at loop-holes,
The women gathering stray wisps from their napes
— Baggy amphibians play a sombre chess
And in at the bright window something gapes.

– Bruce Dawe

The Frogs

They uncoil their springs in sudden leaps.

They jump up from the grass like heavy drops of frying oil.

They settle down, like bronze paper weights, on the wide leaves of the water lily.

One of them is gulping air. You feel like putting a coin in his mouth for the penny bank in his belly.

They come up from the ooze like sighs.

Motionless, they resemble bulging eyes at water level, tumors on the flat pond.

Sitting cross-legged and stupefied, they yawn at the setting sun.

Then, like newsboys filling the street with noise, they cry out the last news of the day.

They're having a party this evening: do you hear them rinsing their glasses?

– Jules Renard

The Brown Frog

To-day as I went out to play
I saw a brown frog in the way,
I know that frogs are smooth and green,
But this was brown — what could it mean?
I asked a lady in the road;
She said it was a spotted toad!

– Mary K. Robinson

St. Benno and the Frog

... It was often the habit of the man of God to go
about the fields in meditation and prayer: and
once as he passed by a certain marsh, a talkative
frog was croaking in its slimy waters: and lest it
should disturb his contemplation, he bade it to be
a Seraphian, inasmuch as all the frogs in Seraphus
are mute. But when he had gone on a little way,
he called to mind the saying in Daniel: "O ye
whales and and all that move in the waters, bless
ye the Lord. O all ye beasts and cattle, bless ye the
Lord." And fearing lest the singing of the frogs
might perchance be more agreeable to God than
his own praying, he again issued his command to
them, that they should praise God in their
accustomed fashion: and soon the air and the
fields were vehement with their conversation.

– *Beasts and Saints,* translated from the Latin by Helen
Waddell

Mutual Respect

Hopping frog, hop here and be seen,
  I'll not pelt you with stick or stone:
Your cap is laced and your coat is green;
  Good bye, we'll let each other alone.

– Christina Rossetti

Grandfather Frog

Fat green frog sits by the pond,
Big frog, bull frog, grandfather frog.
Croak-croak-croak.
Shuts his eye, opens his eye,
Rolls his eye, winks his eye,
Waiting for
A little fat fly.

Croak, croak.
I go walking down by the pond,
I want to see the big green frog,
I want to stare right into his eye,
Rolling, winking, funny old eye.
But oh! he hears me coming by.
Croak-croak-
SPLASH!

– Louise Seaman Bechtel

The Frogs of Windham

Windham resembles Rumford, and stands on Willimantic River. Its meeting-house is elegant, and has a steeple, bell, and clock. Its court-house is scarcely to be looked upon as an ornament. The township forms four parishes, and is ten miles square. Strangers are very much terrified at the hideous noise made on summer evenings by the vast number of frogs in the brooks and ponds. There are about thirty different voices among them; some of which resemble the bellowing of a bull. The owls and whip-poor-wills complete the rough concert, which may be heard several miles. Persons accustomed to such serenaders are not disturbed by them at their proper stations; but one night, in July, 1758, the frogs of an artificial pond, three miles square, and about five from Windham, finding the water dried up, left the place in a body, and marched, or rather hopped, towards Willimantic River. They were under the necessity of taking the road and going through the town, which they entered about midnight. The bullfrogs were the leaders, and the pipers followed without number. They filled a road forty yards wide for four miles in length, and were for several hours, in passing through the town, unusually clamorous. The inhabitants were equally perplexed and frightened; some expected to find an army of French and Indians; others feared an earthquake, and dissolution of nature. The consternation was universal. Old and young, male and female, fled naked from their beds with more shriekings than those of the frogs. The event was fatal to several women. The men, after a flight of half a mile, in which they met with many broken shins, finding no enemies

in pursuit of them, made a halt, and summoned resolution enough to venture back to their wives and children; when they distinctly heard from the enemy's camp these words, Wight, Hilderken, Dier, Pete. This last they thought

meant treaty; and plucking up courage, they sent a triumvirate to capitulate with the supposed French and Indians. These three men approached in their shirts, and begged to speak with the general; but it being dark, and no

answer given, they were sorely agitated for some time betwixt hope and fear; at length, however, they discovered that the dreaded inimical army was an army of thirsty frogs, going to the river for a little water. Such an incursion was never known before nor since; and yet the people of Windham have been ridiculed for their timidity on this occasion. I verily believe an army under the Duke of Marlborough would, under like circumstances, have acted no better than they did.

– Doctor Samuel Peters

The Frog Catcher

If you want to catch a ginu-wine Yankee, you must take a trip up to the State of Vermont. There they shoot up like weeds, generally ranging from six to seven feet in stature. The bait at which they snap is a "great bargain," and a tinman's cart is the only show-box in which they are willing to be exhibited. Mathews, who took his Yankee from Kentucky, made as great a bull as the old Frenchman, that hired an Irish servant to teach him the English pronunciation.

Once upon a time, there lived in a town in Vermont, a little whipper-snapper of a fellow, named Timothy Drew. Timmy was not more than five feet one, in his thick-soled boots. When standing by the side of his tall neighbors, he appeared like a dwarf, among giants. Tall people are too apt to look down on those of less dimensions. Thus did the long-legged Yankees hector poor Timmy for not being a greater man. But what our hero wanted in bulk, he made up in spirit. This is generally the case with small men. As for Timmy, he was "all pluck and gristle!" No steel trap was smarter!

How such a little one grew on the Green Mountains, was always a mystery. Whether he was actually raised there, is indeed uncertain. Some say he was of Canadian descent, and was brought to the States by a Vermont peddler, who took him in barter for wooden cucumber seeds. But Timmy was above following the cart. He disliked trade, as too precarious a calling, and preferred a mechanic art. Though small, Timmy always knew which side of his bread had butter on it. Let it not be supposed that Timothy Drew always put up with coarse gibes at his size. On necessary occasions he was "chock full of fight." To be sure, he could not strike higher than the abdomen of his associates; but his blows were so rapid that he beat out the daylights of a ten-footer before one could say "Jack Robinson." A threat from Timmy was enough. How many belligerents have been quelled by this expressive admonition, "If you say that 'ere again, I'll knock you into the middle of next week!" This occurred in Timmy's younger days. Age cooled his transports, and taught him to endure. He thought it beneath the dignity of an old man to quarrel with idle striplings.

Timmy Drew was a natural shoemaker. No man could hammer out a piece of sole-leather with such expedition. He used his knee for a lap-stone, and by dint of thumping, it became as hard and stiff as an iron hinge. Timmy's shop was situated near the foot of a pleasant valley on the edge of a pond, above which thousands of water lilies lifted their snowy heads. In the spring, it was a fashionable watering-place for bullfrogs, who gathered there from all parts, to spend the warm season. Many of these were of extraordinary size, and they drew near his shop, raised their heads, and swelled out their throats like bladders, until the welkin rang with their music. Timmy, engaged at his work, beat time for them with his hammer, and the hours passed away as pleasantly as the day is long.

Timmy Drew was not one of those shoemakers that eternally stick to their bench like a ball of wax. It was always his rule to carry his work to the dwellings of his customers, to make sure of the fit. On his way home, he usually stopped at the tavern to inquire the news, and take a drop of something to drink. Here it was that the wags fastened upon him with their jokes, and often made him feel as uncomfortable as a short-tailed horse in fly-time. Still Timmy loved to sit in the bar, and talk with the company, which generally consisted of jolly peddlers, recruiting from the fatigues of the last cruise. With such society much was to be learned, and Timmy listened with intense curiosity to their long-spun tales of the wonderful and wild. There is no person that can describe an incredible fact with greater plausibility than a Yankee peddler. His difficult profession teaches him to preserve an iron gravity in expatiating on his wares, which in few cases can be said to recommend themselves. Thus, narratives, sufficient to embarrass the speech of any other relater, carry with them conviction, when soberly received from such a respectable source.

These peddlers took great delight in imposing on the credulity of Timmy Drew. Some of the stories stuffed into his ears were astonishing. One man had been to the South, and gave a marvellous account of the alligators. He had seen one scampering into the water with a full grown negro in his mouth. Another told a story of a great Canadian Giant that weighed 1250 lbs. in his stockings. Another had seen in Boston the Living Skeleton, with ribs as bare as a gridiron. A fourth had been to New York, and described the great Anaconda, which made nothing of mouthing a live goat for its breakfast. A fifth enlarged on the size of the Shark, "which swallowed Mr. Joseph Blaney, as exhibited by his son." The wonderful leaps of Sam Patch lost nothing in their recital here; and the mysterious Sea Serpent, not more than one hundred yards long in Boston, was drawn out to double that length in being trailed up to Vermont behind a tinman's cart. One peddler told what

great smokers the people were in the city of New Orleans. Said he, "The very mosquitoes flit about the streets in the night with cigars in their mouths!" "Yes," replied another, "and what mosquitoes they are! By the living hoky! I have seen them flying around as big as a goose, with a brick-bat under their wings to sharpen their stings on!"

It would be impossible to repeat all the jokes played off on the poor shoemaker. The standing jest, however, was on his diminutive stature, which never was more conspicuous than in their company, for most of them were as tall as bean poles. On this subject, Timmy once gave them a memorable retort. Half a dozen of the party were sitting by the fire, when our hero entered the room. He sat down, but they affected to overlook him. This goaded Timmy, and he preserved a moody silence. Presently one of them spoke.

"I wonder what has become of little Timmy Drew? I have'n't seen that are fellow for a week. By gosh! the frogs must have chawed him up?"

"If he was sitting here before your eyes, you wouldn't see him," said another, "he's so darnation small."

Timmy began to grow uneasy.

"I snaggers," said another, "no more you wouldn't; for he isn't knee high to a toad. I called t'other day at his shop to get my new boots; but I couldn't see nobody in the place. Then I heard something scratching in a corner like a rat. I went to take up a boot, and I heard Timmy sing out, 'Halloo!' 'Where the dickins are you?' said I. 'Here,' said Timmy, 'in this 'ere boot'; and, I snaggers, there he was, sure enough, in the bottom of the boot, rasping off a peg!"

A general roar of laughter brought Timmy on his legs. His dander was raised. "You boast of your bulk," said he, straining up to his full height, and looking contemptuously around; "why, I am like a four-penny bit among six cents — worth the whole of ye!"

I shall now describe a melancholy joke, which they played off on the unfortunate shoemaker; — I say melancholy, for so it proved to him.

A fashionable tailor in a neighboring village came out with a flaming advertisement, which was pasted up in the bar-room of the tavern, and excited general attention. He purported to have for sale a splendid assortment of coats, pantaloons, and waistcoats, of all colours and fashions; also a great variety of trimmings, such as tape, thread, buckram, frogs, button moulds, and all the endless small articles that make up a tailor's stock.

The next time Timmy made his appearance, they pointed out to him the advertisement. They especially called his attention to the article of "frogs," and reminded him of the great quantity to

be caught in Lily Pond. "Why, Timmy," said they, "if you would give up shoemaking and take to frog-catching, you would make your tarnal fortune!"

"Yes, Timmy," said another, "you might bag a thousand in a half a day, and folks say they will bring a dollar a hundred."

"Two for a cent a-piece, they brought in New York, when I was there last," said a cross-eyed fellow, tipping the wink.

"There's frogs enough in Lily Pond," said Timmy; "but it's darnation hard work to catch 'em. I swaggers! I chased one nearly half a day before I took him — he jumped like a grasshopper. I wanted him for bait. They're plaguy slippery fellows."

"Never mind, Timmy, take a fish net, and scoop 'em up. You must have 'em alive, and fresh. A lot at this time would fetch a great price."

"I'll tell you what, Timmy," said one of them, taking him aside, "I'll go you shares. Say nothing about it to nobody. To-morrow night, I'll come and help you catch 'em, and we'll divide the gain." Timmy was in raptures.

As Timmy walked home that night, one of those lucky thoughts came into his head, which are always the offspring of solitude and reflection. Thought he, "These 'ere frogs in a manner belong to me, since my shop stands nearest the pond. Why should I make two bites at a cherry, and divide profits with Joe Gawky? By gravy! I'll get up early to-morrow morning, catch the frogs, and be off with them to the tailor's before sunrise, and so keep all the money myself."

Timmy was awake with the lark. Never before was there such a stir amongst the frogs of Lily Pond. But they were taken by surprise. With infinite difficulty he filled his bag, and departed on his journey.

Mr. Buckram, the tailor, was an elderly gentleman, very nervous and very peevish. He was extremely nice in his dress, and prided himself on keeping his shop as neat as wax-work. In his manner he was grave and abrupt, and in countenance severe. I can see him now, handling his shears with all the solemnity of a magistrate, with spectacles on nose, and prodigious ruffles puffing from his bosom.

He was thus engaged, one pleasant spring morning, when a short stubbed fellow, with a bag on his shoulder, entered the shop. The old gentleman was absorbed in his employment, and did not notice his visitor. But his inattention was ascribed by Timmy to deafness, and he approached and applied his mouth to the tailor's ear, exclaiming, — "I say, mister, do you want any frogs today?"

The old gentleman dropped his shears, and sprung back in astonishment and alarm. "Do you want any frogs this morning?" shouted Timmy, at the top of his voice.

"No!" said the tailor, eyeing him over his spectacles, as if doubting whether he was a fool or madman.

"I have got a fine lot here," rejoined Timmy, shaking his bag. "They are jest from the pond, and as lively as kittens."

"Don't bellow in my ears," said the old man pettishly, "I am not deaf. Tell me what you want, and begone!"

"I want to sell you these 'ere frogs, old gentleman. You shall have them at a bargain. Only one dollar a hundred. I won't take a cent less. Do you want them?"

The old man now got a glance at the frogs, and was sensible it was an attempt at imposition. He trembled with passion. "No!" exclaimed he, "get out of my shop, you rascal!"

"I say you do want 'em," said Timmy, bristling up. "I know you want 'em; but you're playing offish like, to beat down the price. I won't take a mill less. Will you have them, or not, old man?"

"Scoundrel!" shouted the enraged tailor, "get out of my shop this minute!"

Puzzled, mortified, and angry, Timmy slowly turned on his heel and withdrew. "He won't buy them," thought he, "for what they are worth, and as for taking nothing for them, I won't. And yet, I don't want to lug them back again; but if I ever plague myself by catching frogs again, may I be buttered! Curse the old curmudgeon! I'll try him once more." And he again entered the shop.

"I say, Mr. Buckram, are you willing to give me any thing for these 'ere frogs?" The old man was now goaded past endurance. Stamping with rage, he seized his great shears to beat out the speaker's brains.

"Well, then," said Timmy, bitterly, "take 'em among ye for nothing," at the same time emptying the contents of his bag on the floor, and marching out.

Imagine the scene that followed! One hundred live bullfrogs emptied upon the floor of a tailor's shop! It was a subject for the pencil of Cruikshank. Some jumped this way and some that way, and some under the bench and some upon it, some into the fire-place and some behind the door. Every nook and corner of the shop was occupied in an instant. Such a spectacle was never seen before. The old man was nearly distracted. He rent his hair, and stamped in a paroxysm of rage. Then seizing a broom, he made vain endeavors to sweep them out at the door. But they were as contrary as hogs, and when he swept one way,

93

they jumped another. He tried to catch them with his hands, but they were as slippery as eels, and passed through his fingers. It was enough to exhaust the patience of Job. The neighbors, seeing Mr. Buckram sweeping frogs out of his shop, gathered round in amazement, to inquire if they were about to be beset with the plagues of Egypt. But Old Buckram was in such a passion that he could not answer a word, and they were afraid to venture within the reach of his broom. It is astonishing what talk the incident made in the village. Not even the far-famed frogs of Windham excited more. Thus were the golden visions of the frog catcher resolved into thin air. How many speculators have been equally disappointed!

After this affair, Timothy Drew could never endure the sight of a bullfrog. Whether he discovered the joke that had been played upon him, is uncertain. He was unwilling to converse on the subject. His irritability when it was mentioned only provoked inquiry. People were continually vexing him with questions. "Well, Timmy, how goes the frog market?" "How do you sell frogs?" Even the children would call after him, as he passed, "There goes the frog catcher!" Some mischievous person went so far as to disfigure his sign, so that it read:

> SHOES MENDED,
> AND FROGS CAUGHT,
> BY T. DREW.

In fine, Timmy was kept in a continual fever, and the sound of a frog grew hateful to his ears; so that when they tuned up, he would frequently rush out of his shop and pelt them with stones. He could not sleep in his bed. Their dismal croak tormented him through the watches of the night. To his distempered fancy, they often repeated his name in their doleful concerts, thus:

Solo.   Timmy Drew-o-o-o-
           Timmy Drew-o-o-o-
Chorus. Boo-o-boo-o-
          Boo-o-boo-o.

One night he was awaked from a sound sleep, by a tremendous bellowing close under his windows. It seemed as if all the bulls of Bashan were clearing out their throats for a general roar. He listened with amazement, and distinguished the following sounds:

Boo-o-o-o-o-
Timmy Drew-o-o-o-
I can make a shoe-o-o-o-
As well as you-o-o-o-
And better too,-o-o-o-
And better too,-o-o-o-
Boo-o-o-o-

Timmy was certain no common frogs could pipe at this rate. He sprang out of bed, hurried on his clothes, and rushed out of the house. "I'll teach the rascally boys to come here and shout in this manner," said he. But no boys could be seen. It was a clear bright night, all was solitary and still, except a discontented muttering of the sleepless frogs in their uncomfortable bed. Timmy, after throwing a few stones into the bushes, retired, concluding it was all a dream. For a time the stillness continued, when again the terrible concert swelled on the evening breeze for a while, and then gradually sunk away in the distance, thus:

I can make a shoe-o-o-o-
As well as you-o-o-o-
And better too-o-o-o-
Boo-o-o-o-o-
Boo-o-o-
Bo-o-

At last their mysterious concerts became very frequent, and the poor shoemaker was nearly deprived of sleep. In vain did he attempt to discover the authors of the annoyances. They could not be found; so that he naturally began to think it was indeed made by the frogs, and that he was to be haunted in this manner all his remaining days. This melancholy idea became seated in his

mind, and made him miserable. "Ah!" he said to himself, "that was an unlucky day when I disturbed such a frog's nest for that old rascal of a tailor. But it can't be helped."

The next time Timmy Drew stopped at the tavern, he found the people in earnest consultation.

"There he comes," said one, as soon as the shoemaker entered.

"Have you heard the news?" all inquired in a breath.

"No," said Timmy, with a groan.

"Joe Gawky has seen such a critter in the pond! A monstrous great frog, as big as an ox, with eyes as large as a horse's! I never heard of no such thing in my born days!"

"Nor I," said Sam Greening.

"Nor I," said Josh Whiting.

"Nor I," said Tom Bizbee.

"I have heard say of such a critter in Ohio," said Eb Crawly. "Frogs have been seen there, as big as a sucking pig; but not in these 'ere parts."

"Mrs. Timmins," said Sam Greening, "feels quite melancholy about it. She guesses as how it's a sign of some terrible thing that's going to happen."

"I was fishing for pickerel," said Joe Gawky, who, by the by, was a tall spindle-shanked fellow, with a white head, and who stooped in his chest like a crook-necked squash, — "I was after pickerel, and had a frog's hind leg for bait. There was a tarnation great pickerel just springing at the line, when out sailed this great he-devil from under the bank. By the living hoky! he was as large as a small sized man! Such a straddle-bug I never seed! I up lines, and cleared out like a whitehead!"

Timmy examined the faces of the company, and saw that they all credited the story. He began to feel alarmed.

"That are must be the critter I heard t'other night in the pond," said Josh Whiting. "I swanny! he roared louder than a bull."

This extraordinary narrative made a great impression on Timothy Drew. He foresaw something terrible was going to happen. In vain was he questioned touching his knowledge of the monster. He would not say a word.

After this introduction the conversation naturally took a supernatural turn. Every one had some mysterious tale to relate; and thus the evening wore away. Ghosts, witches, and hobgoblins formed prolific themes of discussion. Some told of strange sounds which had been heard in the depths of the forests at midnight; and others of the shapeless monsters which seamen had beheld in the wilderness of the deep. By

degrees the company fell off, one by one, until Timothy Drew found himself alone. He was startled at the discovery, and felt the necessity of departing; yet some invisible power seemed to dissuade him from the step. A presentiment of some coming evil hung like an incubus upon his imagination, and nearly deprived him of strength.

At length, he tore himself away. His course lay over a solitary road, darkened by overshadowing trees. A sepulchral stillness pervaded the scene, which was disturbed only by his echoing footsteps. Onward he glided with stealthy paces, not daring to look behind, yet dreading to proceed. At last he reached the summit of a hill, at the foot of which arose his humble dwelling. The boding cry of the frogs was now faintly heard at a distance. He had nearly reached the door of his shop, when a sudden rustle of the leaves by the side of the pond, brought his heart into his mouth. At this moment, the moon partly emerged from a cloud, and disclosed an object before him that fixed him to the spot. An unearthly monster, in the shape of a mammoth bullfrog, sat glaring upon him with eyes like burning coals. With a single leap, it was by his side, and he felt one of his ankles in its cold rude grasp. Terror gave him strength. With an Herculian effort he disengaged his limb from the monster's clutches, rushed up the hill, and in an instant was gone.

"By the living hoky!" said Joe Gawky, slowly rising from the ground, and arranging his dress, "who'd have guessed this 'ere old pumpkin-head, with a candle in it, would have set that are fellow's stiff knee agoing at that rate! I couldn't see him travel off, for dust."

It is hardly necessary to add that Varmount never seed no more of the Frog Catcher.

– Henry J. Finn, 1831

6 Private Lives of Frogs

A drop of rain!
The frog
Wiped his forehead
With his wrist.

– Kyokusui

The Sound of Frogs

*" . . . a wild, mad, maddening, corybantic,
croaking and creaking orgasm of sound"*
When Leonard Woolf, later to become the
husband of Virginia, was working in Ceylon the
Monsoons arrived, piped in by a chorus of ecstatic
frogs. "The ditches were rushing rivers; the ponds
were full, the earth was already turning green, the
swish of the rain upon the trees was terrific; but
deafening, drowning all other noises was the
ecstatic chorus of millions of frogs from every
ditch and pond and field and compound, a wild,
mad, maddening, corybantic, croaking and
creaking orgasm of sound of wet, wallowing
frogs."

These frogs were no doubt pleased at the
downpour but chances are their passionate vocal
efforts were motivated by another subject near and
dear to their hearts — sex. Most frog sounds are
made by the males to attract females. When the
males gather to call in choruses, they are in reality
forming leks similar to those of birds. The sounds
of the group carry much farther and can be
sustained more continuously than those of a lone
male. A member of a chorus presumably has a
better chance of mating than if he were singing
elsewhere, alone and in competition with the
group. Choruses are typically formed by species
that breed in rain pools and bodies of fresh water
temporarily swollen by rain. They produce some
of the most spectacular sounds of nature. The
wailing of thousands of frogs in a Florida roadside
ditch, in the pitch-black darkness of a hot summer
night, brings to mind the lower levels of the
Inferno. Choruses of South American frogs
sometimes consist of bedlamlike mixtures of ten or
more species.

*"Sounds to banish all disagreeable thoughts or to
die of melancholy."*
In the 18th century, Linnaeus, the Swedish
naturalist, observed that "German frogs croaked 3
or 4 times more loudly than Swedish
frogs — some sang so beautifully it cheered the
heart and banished all disagreeable thoughts,
others so mournfully that one almost died of
melancholy."

*"Pip, poo, ah, drack, jwah, pst, tit, kraw, pé,
tschw, tang, grau, wah, trint and coo"*
Doris M. Cochran of the Smithsonian Institution
spent many nights deep in the steaming jungles of
southeastern Brazil, listening to and describing the
sounds of the frogs:

- Beginning with a roll, a p-r-r-r, then a soft
  whistle repeated half a dozen times in a very
  high pitch.
- Like a cricket — pip-pip-pip-pip.
- Very high pitched poo-poo-poo-poo-
  poo-poo-poo-poo.
- Cry as in ah, ah, ah, grunting like a pig
  slowly.
- Krack, krack, krack, krack, somewhat like a
  hen cackling.
- A booming metallic sound, with regular
  clanging, like that of a blacksmith beating an
  anvil.
- Two strong, high-pitched notes jwah, jwah,
  followed by a low gutteral aw.
- Chirping pst, -pst, -pst often repeated.
- Frequently repeated tit-tit-tit-tit.
- Can be imitated by making a sucking,
  clucking noise with the tongue, many times
  repeated.
- Raucous kraw, kraw, kraw.
- High-pitched crack, crack, crack, crack,
  sounding like a duck.
- Like a sound made winding a watch, cr, cr, cr,
  with a trilled r.

- Interrupted, staccato series of short, sharp trills, very high in pitch that can be imitated by whistling pé-pé, pé-pé into a glass vial.
- A whispering voice, a note like tschw, tschw, tschw, often repeated.
- Begins with tang, tang followed by a continuous crrrrr as if someone was filing iron.
- carara, carara, rough and loud.
- Begins with a tang, followed by chirping like a cicada.
- Repeated creck-creck-creck or strong, hoarse, crau, cr-ren, cr-ren.
- A long rasping sound followed by 2 or 3 clucking notes.
- Hoarse cawing note — grau, grau.
- Cry of wah, wah, wah, wah, wah.
- Grunting ah, ah, ah, ah, repeatedly in a harsh, low voice.
- A p-r-r-r-r, the last very sharply staccato, the first trilled.
- A long distinct whistle, rapid at first, then slow as ---- ----- -----.
- trint-trint-trint-trint.
- Musical high-pitched metallic coo-coo, twice repeated.
- A plaintive whimpering.

North American frogs tend to be loud and aggressive, particularly the male bullfrog (*Rana catesbeiana*). When he isn't croaking for lustful reasons the bullfrog is vocally asserting his territorial imperative. At dusk they leave their shoreline retreats and take up calling stations in open water where they adopt an imperialistic high floating position by inflating the lungs completely with air. Then they proceed to bellow in stereo by expending air through a pair of vocal sacs in the mouth. This process exposes a brilliant yellow patch on the throat which serves as a no trespassing sign. The bullfrog usually lays claim to a 6 meter area and will defend it against other males by wrestling them into submission. He abruptly changes his tune should an invader prove to be of the opposite sex and wrestling of another sort commences. When bullfrogs are mating (in amplexus) they sometimes stay in that position for up to a week.

Whatever their reasons the bullfrogs in Walden Pond seem quite sociable, according to this account by Henry David Thoreau:

"All the shore rang with the trump of bullfrogs, the sturdy spirits of ancient wine-bibbers and wassailers, still unrepentant, trying to sing a catch in their Stygian lake — if the Walden nymphs will pardon the comparison, for though there are almost no weeds, there are frogs there — who would fain keep up the hilarious rules of their old festal tables, though their voices have waxed hoarse and solemnly grave, mocking at mirth, and the wine has lost its flavor, and become only liquor to distend their paunches, and sweet intoxication never comes to drown the memory of the past, but mere saturation and waterloggedness and distention. The most aldermanic, with his chin upon a heart-leaf, which serves for a napkin to his drooling chaps, under this northern shore quaffs a deep draught of the once scorned water, and passes round the cup with the ejaculation tr-r-r-oonk, tr-r-r-onk, tr-r-r-onk! and straightway comes over the water from some distant cove the same password repeated, where the next in seniority and girth has gulped down to his mark; and when this observance has made the circuit of the shores, then ejaculates the master of ceremonies, with satisfaction, tr-r-r-oonk! and each in his turn repeats the same down to the least distended, leakiest, and flabbiest paunched, that there be no mistake; and then the bowl goes round again and again, until the sun disperses the morning mist, and only the patriarch is not under the pond, but vainly bellowing troonk from time to time, and pausing for a reply."

Frog Cantata

people greenery
splash splash

webbed mystics
applaud

spider's holy
brail pollutions
of happiness

trek the winners
from the sun's
tawny musette

war beetles & dragon
flies   jig on circles
of silver   noon's low
menagerie   chatter

shadows dissuade
shades of tomorrow
from the low baptism

where bubbles ask no questions
where there's no redemption
hoppers implode
private cantata

– Joe Rosenblatt

Beethoven: Spring Sonata

(First Impression)

millions of frogs arising.
heading for blue silk moon light. arising. rising. rising.
   li- lululu li- lululu
   lila lila lila
   danglingly dangling legs. rising. rising.

one and another.
up from vast green field surface.
crippled rising rising as cripples.

   shooooooooooooooooooooooot
   shooooooooooooooooooooooot
   shooooooooooooooooooooooot

all in all transparently.
legs extended rising.
from atop one by one drops of sapphire falling.
   glee-kep glee-kep
   glee-kep

all at once laughing together.
laughing. laughing. rising. rising.

   !!!!!!!!!!!!!!!!!!!!!!!
   !!!!!!!!!!!!!!!!!!!!!!!
   !!!!!!!!!!!!!!!!!!!!!!!

things nearing moon dimly heard tho.
green fields with choir of heaven eyes about to burst.

from mountain edge to vast field surface.
levels of air varying shifting dreadfully.

madly believing may night.
millions of frogs arising.

heading for blue silken full moon heading for adventure's dream. heading for light.
rising. rising. rising. rising. rising. rising. rising. rising.

   li- lululu li- lululu
   lila lila lila
   li- lululu li- lululu

   !!!!!!!!!!!!!!!!!!!!!!!
   !!!!!!!!!!!!!!!!!!!!!!!
   !!!!!!!!!!!!!!!!!!!!!!!
   !!!!!!!!!!!!!!!!!!!!!!!

– Kusano Shimpei

The Orator of April

His Mansion in the Pool
The Frog forsakes –
He rises on a Log
And statements makes –
His Auditors two Worlds
Deducting me –
The Orator of April
Is hoarse Today –
His Mittens at his Feet
No Hand hath he –
His eloquence a Bubble
As Fame should be –
Applaud him to discover
To your chagrin
Demosthenes has vanished
In Waters Green –

– Emily Dickinson, untitled poem

Dialogue

Frogs are croakin'
In the valley . . .
Words not spoken
General . . .

Hear them holla
Loud and hearty . . .
Sons of Mallah
At a party . . .

Then their hushing,
Even stranger . . .
Gluttons rushing
To the manger . . .

Ne'er a prop for
Breasts a-bursting . . .
Ne'er a drop for
Throats a-thirsting!

– A Moorish poem, circa 1165

Five Frogs

1st frog A.
ate.
dragon star baby.
glittery.
cotton rain's cotton cloud.

2nd frog O.
me?
i'm king (sd).
mole.
gapin'.

3rd frog L.
seein' hydrangea.
big rainbow color.
ice-cream.

4th frog food-kind.
frog G sd.
airplane seems to be.
copyin' my sound.

5th frog Goros' qay.
likes cannon clouds best.
likes thunder best.
    pour.
    pour.

1st frog &.
2nd frog &.
3rd frog &.
4th frog &.
5th frog &.
    mister sun heaven.
    we earth.
    's song sing.
    -in'.
    kakkun.
    rakkun.
    kokkun.
    yokkun.
    walkin'.
    met a garter snake.
    KYAH!

– Kusano Shimpei

A Frog Sighs

The long sigh of the Frog
Upon a Summer's Day
Enacts intoxication
Upon the Revery –
But his receding Swell
Substantiates a Peace
That makes the Ear inordinate
For corporal release –

– Emily Dickinson, untitled poem

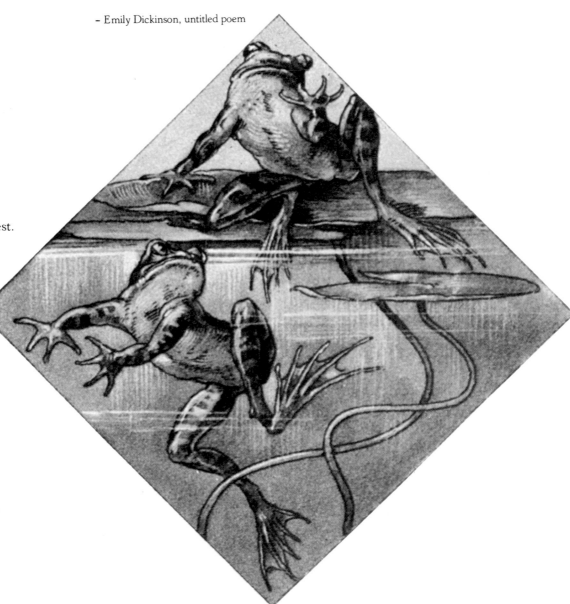

Wood Frogs

Southeast wind. Begins to
sprinkle while I am sitting in
Laurel Glen, listening to hear the
earliest wood frogs croaking. I
think they get under weigh a little
earlier, i.e., you will hear many of
them sooner than you will hear
many hylodes. Now, when the
leaves get to be dry and rustle
under your feet, dried by the
March winds, the peculiar dry
note, wurrk wurrk wur-r-r-k wurk
of the wood frog is heard faintly
by ears on the alert, borne up
from some unseen pool in a
woodland hollow which is open
to the influences of the sun. It is
a singular sound for awakening
Nature to make, associated with
the first warmer days, when you
sit in some sheltered place in the
woods amid the dry leaves. How
moderate on her first awakening,
how little demonstrative! You
may sit half an hour before you
will hear another. You doubt if
the season will be long enough
for such Oriental and luxurious
slowness. But they get on,
nevertheless, and by tomorrow,
or in a day or two, they croak
louder and more frequently. Can
you ever be sure that you have
heard the very first wood frog in
the township croak? Ah! how
weather-wise must he be! There
is no guessing at the weather with
him. He makes the weather in his
degree; he encourages it to be
mild. The weather, what is it but
the temperament of the earth?
and he is wholly of the earth,
sensitive as its skin in which he
lives and of which he is a part.
His life relaxes with the thawing
ground. He pitches and tunes his
voice to chord with the rustling
leaves which the March wind has
dried. Long before the frost is
quite out, he feels the influence of
the spring rains and the warmer
days. His is the very voice of the
weather. He rises and falls like
quicksilver in the thermometer.

You do not perceive the spring so surely in the actions of men, their lives are so artificial. They may make more fire or less in their parlors, and their feelings accordingly are not good thermometers. The frog far away in the wood, that burns no coal nor wood, perceives more surely the general and universal changes.

– Henry David Thoreau (24 March 1859)

All the veneration of Spring connects itself with love
. . . Even the frog and his mate have a new and gayer coat for the occasion.

– Ralph Waldo Emerson

The Common Frog of 1821

It is not necessary to enter into a minute description of an animal so well known as the Frog. Its whole appearance is lively, and its form by no means inelegant. The limbs are well calculated for aiding the peculiar motions of the animal, and its webbed hind feet for assisting its progress in the water, to which it occasionally retires during the heats of summer, and again in the frosts of winter. During the latter period, and till the return of warm weather, it lies in a state of torpor, either deeply plunged in the soft mud at the bottom of stagnant waters, or in the hollows beneath their banks. Immediately on coming forth in the spring, they change their skin, and this operation they repeat, generally about every eight or ten days,

through the whole summer. The old skin, after it is entirely separated from the body, resembles rather a kind of thin mucus, than a membrane.

The spawn of this Frog, which is generally cast in the month of March, consists of a clustered mass of jelly-like transparent, and round eggs, from six hundred to a thousand in number, in the middle of each of which, is contained the embryo or tadpole, in the form of a black speck. This at first sinks to the bottom of the water; but when the eggs begin to enlarge, in consequence of becoming proportionally lighter, it rises to the surface. About the thirty-ninth day, the little animals begin to have motion. They are then so perfectly unlike the Frog in its complete state, that no

person could suppose any relationship existed between them. The Tadpole appears to consist merely of head and tail, the former large, black and roundish, the latter slender and bordered with a broad transparent finny margin. At first it quits the matter in which it was enclosed only occasionally, as if to try its strength, and soon afterwards returns, apparently for the double purpose of retreat and nourishment.

When the animal is about six weeks old, the hind-legs appear, and in about a fortnight, these are succeeded by the fore-legs. The animal now bears a kind of ambiguous appearance, partaking of the form of a Frog and a Lizard. The tail, at this period, begins to decrease, at first very

gradually, and at length so rapidly, as to disappear in the space of a day or two afterwards; the form is then completed, and the animal for the first time, ventures upon land.

With this wonderful change of body, the animals also change their food, and instead of their former vegetable diet, live upon the smaller species of snails, worms, and insects; the structure of their tongue is admirably adapted for seizing and securing this prey. The root is attached to the fore-part of the mouth, so that when unemployed, it lies with the tip towards the throat. The animal by this singular contrivance, is enabled to bend it to a considerable distance out of its mouth. When it is about to seize on any object, it darts it out with great agility, and the prey is secured on its broad and jagged gluey extremity. This it swallows with so instantaneous a motion, that the eye can scarcely follow it. Nothing, however, can appear more awkward than a Frog engaged with a large worm or small snake; for nature seems to have put a restraint upon the voracity of these animals, by forming them very inaptly for seizing and holding their larger prey. Dr. Townson had a large Frog, that one day swallowed in his presence a blind-worm, near a span long, which in its struggles frequently got half its body out again; and when completely swallowed, its contortions were very visible in the flaccid sides of its victor.

About the end of July, when the young Frogs have entirely laid aside their tadpole shape, they quit the water, and soon afterwards emigrate into the woods and meadows. The commencement of their journey is always in the evening. They travel all night, and conceal themselves during the day, under stones, or in other recesses; and resume their journey only when the night begins. In the day time, however, whenever it happens to rain, they always come out of their retreats, as if to refresh themselves in the falling moisture. Mr. Ray informs us, that as he was riding one afternoon in Berkshire, he was much surprised at seeing an immense multitude of Frogs crossing the road. On further examination, he found two or three acres of ground nearly covered with them; they were all proceeding in the same direction, towards some woods and ditches that were before them. He traced them back to the side of a very large pond, which in the spawning-time, he was informed, always so much abounded with Frogs, that their croaking was frequently heard at a great distance.

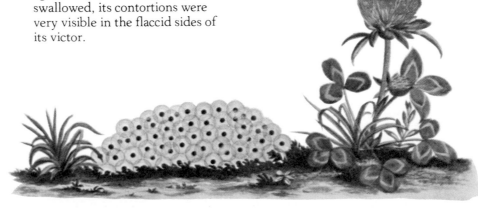

Frogs are numerous throughout Europe, and in the parts about Hudson's Bay, as far north as latitude 61 degrees. They frequent there the margins of lakes, ponds, rivers and swamps; and, as the winter approaches, they burrow under the moss, at a considerable distance from the water, where they remain in a frozen state till

spring. Mr. Hearne says, he has frequently seen them dug up with the moss, frozen as hard as ice. In this state their legs are as easily broken off as the stem of a tobacco-pipe, without giving them the least sensation: but, by wrapping them up in warm skins, and exposing them to a slow fire, they soon come to life, and the mutilated animals gain their usual activity. If, however, they are permitted to freeze again, they are past all recovery. . . .

– *The Natural History of Reptiles and Serpents, 1821*

However singular it may appear, the fact is well ascertained, that Frogs will sometimes fasten upon the backs of fish, so as not to be easily disengaged. Mr. Pennant mentions that in a pond in Dorsetshire, great numbers of Carp were found, each having one of those animals clinging to it; the hind legs were upon the back, and the fore legs attached to the corner of each eye; the Carp also was much wasted away, being teased by its little persecutor.

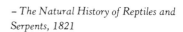

The Evolution of Frog Knowledge

Rane the Frogs are called so because of their croaking voices, for they rattle round the mating ponds and make a row with their exasperating cries. Some frogs are aquatic, some pertain to the marshes, some are called Toads because they live in bramble bushes — and these are larger than the others. Some are called Calamites or Green Frogs, and live among the reeds (*calami*) and little trees. The smallest of all and the greenest are dumb and voiceless. Very small frogs living in dry places or in fields are called Egredulae. Some say that dogs to whom a live frog is given in a lump of food do not bark thereafter.

– A Latin Bestiary of the 12th Century

Of Frogs there are two Kinds; one living both on the Land and in the Water, and common in Marshes, standing Pools, running Streams, and Banks of Rivers, but never in the Sea. The other Sort is frequently in Gardens, Meadows, hollow Rocks, and among Fruits. The Frog in Shape very much resembles a Toad; it is without Venom, and the Female is greater than the Male. The fore Part of the Tongue cleaveth to the Mouth, as in a Fish; the hinder to the Throat, by which it sendeth forth its Voice. It hath two Bladders upon either Side of the Mouth, which it filleth with Wind, and from thence proceedeth the Voice. When it croaketh, it putteth its Head out of the Water, holding the nether Lip even with the Water, and the upper Lip above the Water; and this is the Voice of the Male provoking the Female to Lust.

The hind Legs are very long, which they use in leaping; the fore Legs are shorter, having divided Claws, which are joined together with a thin broad Skin, which helpeth them in swimming. It is said, that Frogs in the Winter-time hide themselves in the Earth, and sometimes they enter into their Holes in Autumn, before Winter, and in the Spring-time come out again.

Their Feet are furnish'd with a little Ball at the end of each Toe, by the singular Contrivance of Nature; that being so supported, they can not only swim, but also walk over the marshy and muddy Waters: They are of a brown, and pale green Colour intermixed together, as if they were water'd with it. These Frogs leave their Spawn on the Banks of the Waters; where such Persons as are curious to observe the Change of these Creatures, gather it, and lay it in an earthen Vessel filled with Water, upon a green Turf, at the bottom: The Spawn or Seed appears as a blackish Point, inclosed in a kind of white Glue; in which it lives, and by degrees increases its Motion, till about the eighth Day; after that they have Tails, and the little things begin to swim in the Water, but they are shapeless young Frogs: In a few Days more their Eyes appear, and a little after their two hind Feet; the two fore Feet likewise coming out of the Skin in about eight Days more: After which their Tails being rotted, drop off; and the Creatures become four-footed, and compleat Frogs, often seen scampering out of the Waters on the Land. But we must observe, that both the Water, and the Turf that the Spawn is put into, must be shifted every now and then; and the little Creatures, as soon as ever we perceive them to move, ought to be nourish'd in the Water with a bit of Bread.

– A Description of a Great Variety of Animals and Vegetables, 1730

7 Symbolism and Meaning of Frogs

*Old pond:
frog jump-in
water sound.*

– Basho

Don't expect too much from a frog

Whenever I feel that I would like to see a frog — and you would be surprised how often that is — I have only to open the door of my living room and take two or three steps to a small pool in the shade of a large spiraea.

Two days after my pool had been filled the first frog had discovered it and taken up permanent residence. Within a week there was at least one individual of the four usual species of this region: the two spotted kinds, Palustris and Pipiens, which most people don't bother to tell apart; Clamitans, the robust fellow with the green neck and head; and Catesbiana, the huge basso profundo who alone has a right to the name "bullfrog." Sometimes these frogs now hide in the herbage or under a stone. Nearly always, however, at least one or two sit on the rough, slab-topped rim of the pool — motionless, unblinking, sublimely confident that sooner or later, but always quite safely in time, some insect will pass by to be snatched up with a lightning tongue. Its unerring, flashing speed is proof enough that the frogs are not unaware of the external world as they sit, seemingly absorbed in meditation, hour after hour. Yet for all that, they are as exempt as the lily from the curse of Adam. They do not work for a living. They do not hunt for food. They do not even sing for their supper. They merely wait for it to pass by and sing afterward.

As the summer rolls along I hope that I may learn something from them as I did from their feathered predecessors. But whatever they may have to teach me will not be as easy to translate into human terms as the lesson of the ducks. Because these last were warm-blooded they were much closer to me in situation and philosophy. Gladness and pain were for us recognizably the same things. They could set me a real example when they rejoiced so unmistakably in the little pool which had to serve them in lieu of a lake. But the frogs are antediluvian. Like me, they are, to be sure, alive, and their protoplasm is much like mine. But they seem strangely cold-blooded in a figurative as well as a literal sense. No doubt they feel the difference between well-being and its reverse; their satisfactions may be, for all I know, as deep or deeper than mine. But their monumental placidity is something which I can hardly hope to achieve.

That is one of the reasons why I like to have them about, why I am acutely aware of the strangeness of having almost at my doorstep these creatures who can demonstrate what to be alive must have meant millions of years ago when the Amphibia were the most progressive, the most adventurous, one is almost tempted to say the most warm-blooded and passionate, of living creatures.

I need do no more than notice the grasshopper just fallen into the pool to realize that, comparatively speaking, the frogs are more like me than I had supposed. At least neither their anatomy nor their ways are as remote from mine as are those of the insects whose tastes and habits sometimes shocked even Henri Fabre with their monstrousness. So far as remoteness of soul is concerned there is at least as much difference between the grasshopper and the frog as between the frog and the duck; perhaps indeed more than between the duck and me. The frog got to be what he is by moving in the direction which was to end — for the time being at least — in me. Even though land insects were newcomers when the frogs were already a well established family they took long ago the direction which was to carry their descendants further and further away from the rest of us; further and further from the frog, the duck, and the man. When I realize that, I feel that Catesbiana and I are not so different, as differences go in this world, as I had thought.

At least one thing which I already knew the frogs have by now taught several visitors who consented to inspect them. Part-time countrymen though all these visitors were, several saw for the first time that the frog, like the toad, is not "ugly and venomous," but "interesting looking." And this I know is halfway to the truth that they are beautiful in their own fashion and ask only that we enlarge our conception of beauty to include one more of nature's many kinds. They are as triumphantly *what* they are as man has ever succeeded in being, and no human imagination could devise a new creature so completely "right" according to the laws of his own structure and being. They are the perfect embodiment of frogginess both outwardly and inwardly, so that nearly every individual achieves, as very few human beings do, what the Greeks would have called his entelechy — the complete realization of the possibilities which he suggests. Frogs are not shadows of an ideal but the ideal itself. There is scarcely one who is not either a froggy Belvedere or a froggy de Milo. To realize this one need only go to frogs as so many critics have told us we

should go to works of art, asking first "What is the intention" and then "How well has this intention been achieved?"

One of my lady visitors after looking for a while at Catesbiana expressed the opinion that he was "cute," and I restrained myself because I recognized that she meant well, that this was even, for her, the first faint beginning of wisdom. I did not ask as I was about to ask if the prehistoric saurians were "cute," if the stretches of geologic time are "nice," and if the forests of the carboniferous age are "sweet." As my frog gazed at both of us with eyes which had seen the first mammalian dawn, lived through thousands of millennia before the first lowly primate appeared and so saw more of the world than all mankind put together, I asked him to forgive the impertinence of this latecomer. The Orientals say that God made the cat in order that man might have the pleasure of petting a tiger. By that logic He must have made frogs so that we can commune with prehistory.

– Joseph Wood Krutch

Frog Omens

- The clamorous croaking of frogs is a sign of rain. (U.S.)
- After frogs first sing in Spring there will be three freezes before Spring weather fairly sets in. (U.S.)
- The sap in the maple trees will stop running when frogs begin to peep in the Spring. (U.S.)
- Whatever one is doing when the first frog is heard in the Spring, the same thing they will be doing much of the year. (New England, U.S.)
- To see a frog with red eyes is a bad omen. (Korea)
- If one kills a frog cows will give bloody milk. (U.S.)
- If you kill a frog warts will come on your hand. (Iran)
- If you kill a frog it will rain for three days. (U.S.)
- If you kill a frog the ghost of the creature will come to you at night and make a hole in your back. (Durham, England)
- Meeting a frog in the road on the way to a dice game is extremely good luck. (U.S.)
- It is extremely lucky to meet up with a frog . . . money follows the frog into your hands. (Southern U.S.)

- If you see seven frogs at one time in a pond, you will soon be wealthy.
- If the first frog you see in Spring leaps in water and not on land, you will experience misfortunes all that year.
- If the first frog that you see in the Spring is sitting on dry ground, it signifies that during the same year you will shed as many tears as the frog would require to swim away in.
- If you see the first frog on the edge of a pond, you may expect a dry Summer.
- A frog on the walk on a dry day is a sure sign of rain.
- When the frogs in the grass appear of a bright yellowish green, the weather will be fine; but if they are dark and dirty, the rain will come.
- The Welsh say that if an Irishman spits on a frog, it will die.
- If frogs are not frozen up three times after they begin to croak, a bad season will follow.
- If you see a frog in January, you will see frost the following day.
- If you see a frog in front of you and it begins to work its mouth, it is counting your teeth, and you must turn away instantly or you will die shortly.
- It is unlucky to see a dead frog in the road.
- A frog coming into the house is bad luck.

The Symbolic Frog

Frogs and Love

Pliny, the Roman author who perished in the eruption of Vesuvius in 79 A.D. had graphic ideas of the frog as a sex object. In his *Natural History* he gives particular directions telling how a husband might make his unfaithful wife take an aversion to her lover, by means of a frog.

The young men of ancient Bohemia made use of frogs to gain the love of young ladies. On St. George's Day a frog was caught, wrapped up in a white cloth, and put onto an ant hill after sunset. The creature croaked terribly while the ants gnawed the flesh from its bones. Finally, all that remained was one small bone in the shape of a hook and another in the shape of a shovel. The aspiring lover then took the hook-shaped bone to the girl of his choice and hooked her dress with it. She immediately fell head over heels in love with him. When he tired of her he had only to touch her with the shovel-shaped bone and her affection would vanish as quickly as it came.

In Derbyshire and other rural counties of medieval England, a girl might regain the affections of her strayed lover by means of a kind of voodoo ceremony performed on a frog. She would stick pins all over a living frog and then bury it. The young man would suffer extreme pain in all his extremities and shortly return to her. She would then dig up the now dead frog and remove the pins whereupon the marriage would take place.

In east Yorkshire a pining young woman could find happiness by means of a variation on the Bohemian frog-bone charm. She would place a pin-stuck frog in a box and leave it there until it was quite dead and withered. Then, removing a small key-shaped bone from the corpse she would secretly fasten it to the man of her choice while saying (somewhat redundantly in the case of the frog):

> I do not want to hurt this
>   frog,
> But my true lover's heart to
>   turn,
> Wishing that he no rest may
>   find,
> Till he come to me and speak
>   his mind.

Shortly thereafter the young man would come to her, suffering the same agony as the frog, and ask her hand in marriage.

As well as playing starring roles in folklore, frogs often miraculously transform into young men in fables and fairy tales. The origins of this maneuver can be seen in a bronze sculpture from Egypt in the British Museum which features a frog on the end of a phallus. Freudians view the frog in the folktale as symbolic of the penis. At first the penis is feared by a woman but once she experiences sexual contact and pleasure, she realizes that the object of her fear is actually something desirable which gives new meaning to the transformation of the ugly frog into a handsome prince in *The Frog Prince*. Their theory is interesting, except that in many variations of the folktale the frog is a woman, recalling its ancient role in mythology and religion.

Frogs and Mortality

Certain cultures attributed human mortality to frogs. The Ekoi tribe in southern Nigeria told a tale of the sky-god Obassi Osaw who one day said to himself: "Men fear to die. They do not know that perhaps they may come to life again. I will tell them that sometimes such a thing may happen, then they will have less dread of death." So he stood up in his house in the sky, and called a frog and a duck before him. To the frog he said, "Go to earth and say to the people, 'When a man dies, it is the end of all things; he shall never live again'." To the duck he said, "Go tell the earth folk that if a man dies he may come to life again." He then showed them the road, saying, "Take my message. Duck, you may go to the left hand. Frog, keep to the right." So the frog kept to the right, and when he came to the earth he delivered his

message of death to the first men he met, telling them that when they died it would be the end of them. In due course the duck also reached the earth, but happening to arrive at a place where the people were making palm oil, she fell to gobbling it up and forgot all about the message of immortality which the good god had charged her to deliver to mankind. That is why men are all mortals down to this day. They are bound to go by the message of the frog, the message from the duck never having arrived.

Another version of this idea reversed the message-sending process and introduced a frog with self-interests. The tribes in Togoland in West Africa believed that a dog was sent to God with a request that when men died they would like to come to life again. Meanwhile a frog took it upon himself to tell God that when men died they would prefer not

to come to life again. The dog became hungry on his journey to God and stopped to eat, thinking that he could easily outrun the frog and arrive at God's doorstep first, thereby enabling men to become immortal. But the frog arrived first and said to the deity: "When men die they would prefer not to come to life again." Just then the dog arrived and said: "When men die they would like to come to life again." God was naturally puzzled, and said to the dog, "I really do not understand these two messages. As I heard the frog's request first, I will comply with it. I will not do what you said." That is the reason why men die and do not come to life again. If the frog had only minded his own business instead of meddling with other people's, the dead would all have come to life again henceforward. But frogs come to life again when it thunders at the beginning of

the rainy season, after they have been dead all the dry season while the Harmattan wind was blowing. Then, while the rain falls and the thunder peals, they can be heard quacking in the marshes. Thus the frog had his own private ends to serve in distorting the message. He gained for himself the immortality of which he robbed mankind.

Frogs and the Weather

Frogs were widely used as charms to draw rain from the heavens. Early Venezuelans regarded the frogs as "Lords of the Waters" and they showed much awe and fear of them. However they weren't above whipping them with sacred switches in time of drought. Pre-Columbian artisans in Central America fashioned stylized frogs from solid gold and placed them on hill tops or wore them as pendants to promote rain. To most North American Indians frog croaking foretold rain but, to the always contrary Iroquois, the frog was a symbol of aridity.

In some parts of south-eastern Australia prone to heavy rainfall, the natives were careful not to molest Tidelek the frog, or Bluk the bullfrog, because they were thought to be full of water instead of intestines. If either of them were injured or killed torrential rains were bound to come. A legend of the area described how a long time ago a frog drank up all the waters in the lakes and rivers, and then sat in the dry reed beds swollen to an enormous size, saying, "Bluk! Bluk!" in a deep gurgling voice. All the other animals wandered about gasping for a drop of moisture, but finding none, they all agreed that they would die of thirst unless they could make the

frog laugh. So they tried one after the other, but for a long time in vain. At last the conger eel and his relations, hung round with lake grass and gay sea-weed, reared themselves on their tails and pranced around the fire. This was too much for the frog. He opened his mouth and laughed till the water ran out and the lakes and streams were full once more.

Frogs and Gods

In ancient Egypt frogs were considered a symbol of female fertility. Scholars believe this is linked with the annual over-flowing of the Nile, so necessary for the continuance of life among the pyramids. In the quagmire of mud left by the receding floods, frogs thrived in huge numbers, heralding the arrival of the growing season. The frog became the symbol of *hefnu*, 100,000 or an immense number. It followed that Heket, the water goddess, should have the head of a frog. The grateful Egyptians wore frogs as a talisman to attract her favours of fruitfulness.

Many Egyptian women wore frog amulets of gold and lesser metals to enlist the aid of Heqit, the midwife goddess. It was she who presided over conception and birth. She was present at the birth of every king of Egypt and assisted Isis in resuscitating Osiris and in making effective her union with him.

In Hermopolis, a city of upper Egypt, a group of eight gods, the sacred Ogdoad, were responsible for creating the world. Four of these deities: Amon, Hekt, Keh and Non, had frog heads. Before long the frog had become one of the principal beings associated with the idea of resurrection, as well as creation, probably because of its alternating periods of appearance and disappearance. Frogs were mummified with the dead and honoured with sculptures in the temple of Thebes where a terra cotta lamp in the form of a frog was found bearing the inscription "I am the resurrection."

The Coptic Sect adopted the frog as a symbol of the Resurrection and sculpted frogs onto their monuments in the catacombs of Alexandria, side by side with the Coptic Cross.

In the eightieth year of the life of Moses in the reign of Pharaoh IV, the frog plague mentioned in Exodus established the anti-frog viewpoint of Christianity. In this, the Fifth of the Ten Plagues sent upon the sinning Egyptians, the waters dry up, the frogs die and rot, giving off noxious odors and causing horrible diseases to descend on all and sundry.

In spite of such dire warnings the worship of frogs persisted even though the powers-that-were in Christianity maintained that frogs had nothing to do with creation or resurrection, but were instead symbols of heresy and those who would snatch at life's fleeting pleasures. The porta della rana (door of the frog) built in 1497 on the cathedral of Como in Italy, features a frog snapping at the fleeting pleasure of an insect. Philaster, Bishop of Brescia, condemned to hell members of the *ranarum cultores* or frog-worshippers and in the year 428 a law was passed forbidding Batrachians (frogs) to reside within the limits of the Roman Empire.

Traces of the frog influence on Christianity survive to this day. In parts of Italy children observe the custom of sounding, in Holy Week and on Easter Eve, a wooden instrument which resembles the croaking of the frog. The ceremony is called *canta rana*: the frog sings.

While Christians banished frogs other doctrines embraced them. In Hebrew antiquity the frog was symbolic of the degraded and timid turning to knowledge and wisdom. In the 103rd hymn in the seventh Mandalam of the Rigvedas, a celestial choir of frogs sings the praise of Indras, the ancient Hindu god. Later they are themselves invoked as deities by the Vedic poet Vasishtha, who compares their croaking to the chanting of Brahmans who are performing sacrificial rites.

In Altai Tatar mythology, the Mohammedan and Turkic tribes blessed the frog as the discoverer of the mountain containing birch and stones from which fire was first made. In China a frog typified the moon and was called

the Heavenly Chicken. Ch'ing-wa Shen — The Frog Spirit — was worshipped by some ancient Chinese for commercial prosperity and the prevention and healing of sickness. These people believed that frog spawn fell from heaven with the dew. In Burmese and Indo-Chinese legend the frog was responsible for the eclipse by swallowing the moon. Frog amulets are sometimes worn today in that part of the world as well as in Italy, Greece and Turkey, to ward off the evil eye.

In Japan frogs were, and still are, the symbol of energy and perseverance. Bullfrogs are considered lucky and are encouraged to enter houses to be fed. They are credited with the power of drawing all mosquitoes out of the room by simply

sucking in their breath. In Japanese folklore the frog is descended from a goblin bullfrog, which sucked in, not insects, but men.

Among Mexican Indians a frog with a blood-stained mouth in every joint in her body was a form of mother goddess who gave birth to mankind and devoured the dead as well as the occasional living person. Women were sacrificed to her at regular intervals. Central American tribes had a variation on this theme featuring a frog goddess with a multitude of udders who was their patroness of childbirth.

Indian tribes on the Pacific coast worshipped Frog Woman who had created earth and had made a gift of metal to them. Frogs are featured in many Indian legends. In "The Man In the Moon" story of the Lillooet tribe, three frog sisters hopped onto his face and can still be seen there on nights of the full moon.

124

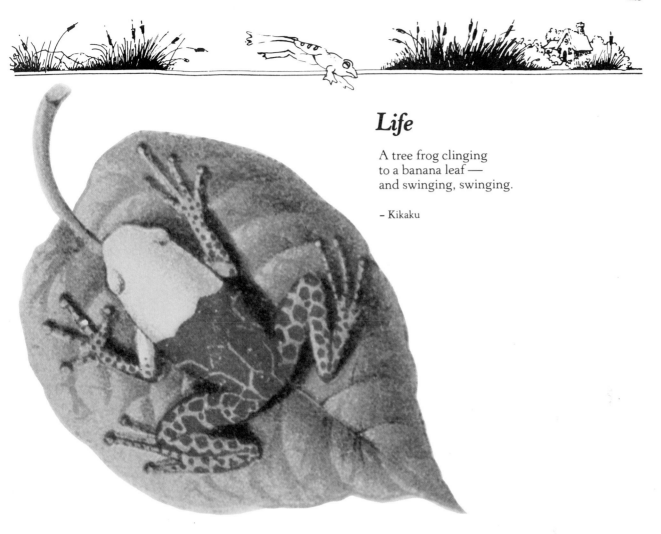

Life

A tree frog clinging
to a banana leaf —
and swinging, swinging.

– Kikaku

Encounter

And when, upon some showery day,
Into a path or public way
A frog leaps out from bordering grass,
Startling the timid as they pass,
Do you observe him, and endeavour
To take the intruder into favour;
Learning from him to find a reason
For a light heart in a dull season.
And you may love him in the pool,
That is for him a happy school,
In which he swims as taught by nature,
Fit pattern for a human creature,
Glancing amid the water bright,
And sending upward sparkling light.

– William Wordsworth

Frogs

Frogs sit more solid
Than anything sits. In mid-leap they are
Parachutists falling
In a free fall. They die on roads
With arms across their chests and
Heads high.

I love frogs that sit
Like Buddha, that fall without
Parachutes, that die
Like Italian tenors.

Above all, I love them because
Pursued in water, they never
Panic so much that they fail
To make stylish triangles
With their ballet dancer's
Legs.

– Norman MacCaig

The Frog

Be kind and tender to the Frog,
And do not call him names,
As 'Slimy skin' or 'Polly-wog,'
Or likewise 'Ugly James,'
Or 'Gap-a-grin,' or 'Toad-gone-wrong,'
Or 'Bill Bandy-knees':
The Frog is justly sensitive
To epithets like these.
No animal will more repay
A treatment kind and fair;
At least so lonely people say
Who keep a frog (and by the way,
They are extremely rare).

– Hilaire Belloc